Cryptocurrency Masterclass 2018

The Ultimate A to Z Guide

Learn how to step in the cryptocoins and master the necessary strategies to trade virtual assets with success

Patrick Wilder

Copyright 2018 by Patrick Wilder - All rights reserved.

This document is geared towards providing exact and reliable information regarding the topic and issue covered. The publication is sold on the idea that the publisher is not required to render an accounting, officially permitted, or otherwise, qualified services. If advice is necessary, legal or professional, a practised individual in the profession should be ordered.

- From a Declaration of Principles which was accepted and approved equally by a Committee of the American Bar Association and a Committee of Publishers and Associations.

In no way is it legal to reproduce, duplicate, or transmit any part of this document by either electronic means or in printed format. Recording of this publication is strictly prohibited, and any storage of this document is not allowed unless with written permission from the publisher. All rights reserved.

The information provided herein is stated to be truthful and consistent, in that any liability, in terms of inattention or otherwise, by any usage or abuse of any policies, processes, or directions contained within is the solitary and utter responsibility of the recipient reader. Under no circumstances will any legal obligation or blame be held against the publisher for any reparation, damages, or monetary loss due to the information herein, either directly or indirectly.

Respective authors own all copyrights not held by the publisher.

The information herein is offered for informational purposes solely and is universal as so. The presentation of the data is without a contract or any type of guarantee assurance.

The trademarks that are used are without any consent, and the publication of the trademark is without permission or backing by the trademark owner. All trademarks and brands within this book are for clarifying purposes only and are the owned by the owners themselves, not affiliated with this document.

Table of Contents

Introduction 9
What is bitcoin? 10
   Wallets 10
   Transactions in the blockchain 11
   Bitcoin miners 12
   Bitcoin mining today 13
   Specifications. 14
Cryptocurrency Glossary for Newcomers 15
   Altcoin 15
   ASIC 15
   Blockchain 16
   Cryptocoin / cryptocurrency 17
   DAO 18
   Digital asset 19
   Difficulty (mining) 19
   Fiat money / currency 20
   Mining 21
   Proof of Stake (POS) 22
   Proof of Work (POW) 23
   Smart Contract 24
   Token 25
Setting up your bitcoin wallet 28
   Desktop wallets 28
Airbitz 28

- Armony 29
- Bitcoin Core 30
- Bitcoin Knots 30
- Bitcoind 31
- Bitcoin Explorer (BX) 31
- Libbitcoin-explorer 32
- Bitcoin Wallet 33
- Blocktrail 33
- Electrum 34
- Gocoin 34
- GreenAddress 35
- MultiBit (no longer supported) 35
- Mycelium 36
- My Wallet 37
  - Mobile wallets 37
- You should always: 39
  - Online wallets 40
  - Exchange services 40
- Coinbase 40
- Bittrex 41
  - Hardware wallets 43
  - Paper wallets 44
  - Memory wallets 44
- Basic bitcoin trading ideas 45
  - Buy or sell? 46
- Alternative cryptocurrencies: The Altcoins 48
- Top 20 cryptocurrencies in the market 50
  - #1 Bitcoin: the original cryptocoin 50

A short story of the Bitcoin 51
  #2 Ethereum 53
A short story of Ethereum 53
  #3 Ripple 55
A short story of Ripple 56
  #4 Bitcoin Cash 57
A short story of Bitcoin Cash 57
  #5 Litecoin 59
A short story of Litecoin 60
  #6 Cardano 61
A short story of Cardano 61
  #7 NEO 62
A short story of NEO 63
  #8 Stellar 64
A short story of Stellar 64
  #9 EOS 65
A short story of EOS 66
  #10 IOTA 67
A short story of IOTA 67
  #11 Dash 68
A short story of Dash 69
  #12 NEM 71
A short story of NEM 71
  #13 Monero 72
A short story of Monero 73
  #14 Lisk 74
A short story of Lisk 74
  #15 TRON 75

A short story of TRON 75
  #16 Ethereum Classic 77
A short story of Ethereum Classic 77
  #17 VeChain 78
A short story of VeChain 78
  #18 Qtum 80
A short story of Qtum 80
  #19 Bitcoin Gold 82
A short story of Bitcoin Gold 82
  #20 Tether 83
A short story of Tether 84
Which cryptocurrency is worth mining in 2018? 85
  What is the price of electricity worldwide? 87
  What to mine? 88
What do you need to mine Bitcoin? 88
Will Bitcoin mining become "more difficult"? 90
What do you need to mine Ethereum? 92
What do you need to mine Ripple? 94
What do you need to mine Bitcoin Cash? 95
What do you need to mine Litecoin? 96
  WhatToMine.com 96
Short roadmap for new bitcoin users 98
Conclusion 100
Appendices 102
  How to create a new Groestlcoin (GRS) standard wallet with the Electrum-GRS 2.5.4 in Windows 10 102
  How to create a new two-step authentication Bitcoin (BTC) wallet with the Electrum 3.0.6 client in Windows 10 109

How to sign up on Coinbase – exchange service for BTC, BCH, ETH, and LTC 127

How to receive BTC, ETH, BCH or LTC tokens on your Coinbase wallet 135

Web 135

iOS 136

Android 136

How to send BTC, ETH, BCH or LTC tokens to another wallet on Coinbase 137

Web 137

iOS 138

QR code 138

Android 139

QR code 139

Introduction

Thank you for your interest in the book, *"The A to Z Cryptocurrency Book"*. This book will open a new world of possibilities in the buoyant bitcoin market. Welcome to the ultimate guide to getting started in the *cryptos*.

This e-book contains current steps and strategies on how to get started in cryptocurrency trading, from signing up for an exchange service to trading virtual assets as any other every day's doing.

Have you heard of the *bitcoin*? Do you want to understand what's going on with this *'crypto'* trend? Then, this is the book you are looking for. From complete newcomer to self-sufficient crypto user once you read this book!

No previous knowledge or experience with the cryptocurrencies is assumed. Thus, this book explains the concepts that are needed to become self-sufficient in the use of any virtual asset.

Ready to become a part of the bitcoin community? Once you master the basics of the cryptocurrencies buy/sell mechanics, it will be like riding a bicycle on a plane surface on a sunny day.

The bitcoin forever changed the way we understand currency transactions less than a decade ago. You can also be part of this growing market. Reading this book is the first step to make it happen.

Thanks again for downloading this book, I hope you enjoy it!

Patrick Wilder

What is bitcoin?

The first *decentralized* currency developed ever was the bitcoin. By the end of 2008, someone[1] known by the nickname of *Satoshi Nakamoto*[2] published an anonymous paper describing this new digital currency system.

A few months later, in early 2009, the first Bitcoin client was released. From that moment, people could mine this virtual asset with their computers. It's a process commonly known as *mining* bitcoins.

So, *what is a bitcoin again?* You can think of the bitcoin as a large *code* stored somewhere. Digital codes could be on your computer, on a remote server or even in an SD card safely stored in a vault. There are those who memorize the codes!

You can also write the code on a piece of paper if you feel like it. Whatever the storing method, you need to secure the private *keys* to access the bitcoins – otherwise the neighbours could use your coins!

However, learning so many codes by heart is quite a challenge!

Wallets

This is when *wallets* come to save the day. The private keys are stored

---

[1] It could also be a group of people provided that the identity behind the nickname is unknown.
[2] Although many have researched about the real identity of this person or dev team, it remains unknow as of today. You can read more about the attempts to unveil this ID here.

in the wallets, which have different types: desktop, mobile, web, paper, and hardware. You can add the memory to this list if you feel mnemotechnical.

In fact, the bitcoins are not on your devices. They are stored within the bitcoin network, a set of servers that allow the transactions with this cryptocurrency. You make use of wallets to buy or sell bitcoins.

To sum up:

- Bitcoins are mined with computers that solve increasingly complex mathematical problems.

- The codes associated with the bitcoins and the private keys to access them are *calculated* with the mining process.

- To ease the use of bitcoins, the private keys are stored in wallets, the digital equivalent of leather wallet for fiat currency.

- The user of the bitcoins needs to access the wallet to buy or sell this cryptocurrency.

Got it? Awesome. Anyone can make use of bitcoins without a complete understanding of the technical details. Though the system may seem confusing for the newcomer, it should not be discouraging.

Transactions in the blockchain

Enters the blockchain. There is a globally shared public ledger which is the basis of the bitcoin network: the blockchain. Every encrypted operation is included in this *register* in chronological order once confirmed.

There is a minimum number of confirmations required to validate a transaction. Currently, most exchange services authorize transactions with six endorsements. For low payments, it is possible to have a blockchain approval with one or two proofs only.

When a transaction occurs, the private keys stored in the wallet mathematically prove that the legitimate owner has accessed the bitcoin. These keys provide a digital signature to the operation.

To summarize:

- A bitcoin transaction is a transfer of value between wallets.
- Each transaction must be validated by users of the bitcoin network to be included in the public ledger, the blockchain.
- Once validated, a transaction cannot be undone or modified.
- The transactions are secured by the wallets private keys.

Sounds safe, right? There are additional security layers to protect your virtual assets. For instance, by default, you need security method to access a bitcoin wallet. It could be a user and a password, or a biometric scan, such as the fingerprint.

Bitcoin miners

Mining is the mathematical process by which computers need to go through to get bitcoins and confirm transactions. This process enforces a chronological order in the blockchain. The operations cannot be undone or altered.

To be confirmed, a transaction must be included in a block: a set of operations which is loaded to the blockchain. A block requires specific encryption to be part of the public ledger.

The process of mining also serves as a lottery. To avoid that anyone could manipulate the blocks, no one is in constant charge of loading them to the blockchain; it is a random rotation within the users.

Likewise, when a new bitcoin is found (calculated), the members who contributed get credit for it, i.e. they can include the private keys into their wallet to have legitimate ownership. During the years, bitcoin mining has become a more technically demanding algorithm.

In fact, nowadays no regular computer can mine bitcoins. You can always run a mining client on your laptop, but it would take ages to earn any bitcoins. So, it is no longer a profitable strategy to mine.

Bitcoin mining today

You need a chip with the optimal specifications to mine bitcoins profitably. The Antminer S9 is the most recent version of the mining device capable of processing the operations at the fastest velocity.

This device has thrice the computation power than its predecessor, the Antminer S7, with a has rate of 14 TH/s. This means it can perform 14 000 000 000 000 operations in the bitcoin network per second.

This optimized device is not yet available in the market but will be released soon. The Antminer S9 has no fewer than 189 chips which work in conjunction to provide the operational power that is required for bitcoin mining.

Besides, this new release is more energy-efficient than the S7. For sure, it will propel the bitcoin miners' capabilities to the stratosphere. Due to the increasing difficulty of the mining process, it is a very expected launch.

Why does the bitcoin mining process become more involved? This is a consequence of the algorithm to find the correct codes that represent bitcoin - which are, in fact, very long numbers with certain

Specifications.

Think of it this way, when the first miners searched for bitcoins; there remain all of them to be found. Nowadays, over 16.8 million out of the 21 million max possible bitcoins have been mined.

Therefore, it is to expect that the search must be more complicated as we get closer to that maximum. There will never be more than 21 million bitcoin tokens because the system does not allow that.

Some experts think that the S7 and the S9 will be in the market for a very long time, provided that their hash rate exceeds by far the capacity of regular PCs.

Talking prices, the S7 ranges from USD500 to USD700, whereas the newest release to come, the S9 is estimated to cost over USD2000. Quite an inversion, but it can turn anyone from a newcomer into a severe miner!

We will study the mining process further in the chapter _Which cryptocurrency is worth mining?_ Moreover, we will also discuss the profit that is expected for the most popular cryptocurrencies as of early 2018.

Cryptocurrency Glossary for Newcomers

To understand the next chapters, you should have a basic comprehension of the most common terms of the cryptocurrency niche. In this section, we explain the standard terms and acronyms which will be of regular use in this book.

Altcoin

Short for alternative coin, this term refers to the cryptocurrencies which came after the bitcoin and is mostly used for those coins which are not mainstream nowadays. When the bitcoin became popular, more decentralized projects were launched. Most of them were based on their own token, the altcoins.

Moreover, the altcoins were developed to solve any of the limitations of the Bitcoin. Altcoins often differ from each other drastically despite the similarities that they could share. In other words, many altcoins are based on the core Bitcoin code, but that is the only similarity.

The most popular cryptocurrencies, e.g. the top 5 or so, are not usually named by this term. Of course, this is not written in stone. The less popular coins are often called altcoins. In fact, any cryptocurrency that was developed after the Bitcoin is a legitimate altcoin, don't you think?

ASIC

The application specific integrated circuit is a custom design for a high-efficiency performance. ASICs are needed to get profitability in the mining process of some cryptocurrencies. The Bitcoin is the most popular coin which demands this kind of powerful devices.

As of now, the most profitable circuit for bitcoin mining purposes is the AntMiner S9, which costs around USD2.400. Using regular computers or GPUs may be so inefficient in the mining that you could get no profit from the activity. You may risk losing money in electricity expenses if you are not using the most efficient device for the task.

The custom operative systems also improve the efficiency of the hardware. For instance, a GPU may develop more computational power with the optimal settings. Hence, both hardware and software are deciding when it comes to mining tokens. An ASIC often demands a high inversion to get started in the quest for tokens.

Blockchain

The core technology which makes it possible to have cryptocurrency networks is this ledger called the blockchain. In a few words, the blockchain is a register which cannot be altered which can record any valuable information in chronological order.

It is a distributed database which does not have the information copied by the member of the network. The main strength of the blockchain is the fact that the register is allocated to every user in the system. Thus, there is no way an attacker could corrupt all the ledgers.

For years, the only way to share documents relied on sending a file. Then, you'd have to wait to receive the edited text back to make changes; then you'd submit the next version, and so on. Hence, both contributors could not make edits on the same text simultaneously with such system.

Then, the cloud services arrive to allow multiple editors to work on the same document at a time. A blockchain is a similar approach which was initially applied to the Bitcoin development. Nowadays, entrepreneurs have realized that this technology can be used to store any valuable information.

Hence, there are several applications based on the blockchain tech being regularly created.

Cryptocoin / cryptocurrency

A digital asset is designed to work as a medium of exchange based on cryptography to assure the security of the transactions. The creation of new coin units and the authentication of the transactions are secured with cryptographic algorithms.

In 2009, the Bitcoin was the first decentralized currency of this nature. Since then, many cryptocurrencies have been deployed, most of them are usually referred to as altcoins. Any cryptocurrency must comply with these conditions to be acknowledged in this category:

1. No central regulating authority. Distributed consensus to take decisions about the ecosystem.

2. Overview of the cryptocurrency tokens, the issue and the ownership within the system.

3. The creation of new cryptocurrency units is regulated by the system. The terms of the issue and the ownership of the new tokens are under the system control.

4. Only a cryptographical process is valid to prove the ownership and the authenticity of the cryptocurrency tokens in the system.

5. Cryptocurrency token transactions which change the

ownership of the cryptocoin units are possible within the system. Only an entity with authentic ownership of the tokens can create a transaction statement which involves those cryptocoin units.

6. The system has measures to avoid double spends. Whenever two simultaneous instructions concerning the same cryptocurrency tokens occur, only one of them will be performed.

All the cryptocurrency ecosystems comply with the above six conditions. The specific measures and procedures change from one cryptocoin system to another, though. Besides, the most recent blockchain developments have introduced features to enhance the compliance with those conditions, e.g. to improve the token issue (though mining or other means) or to avoid double spends.

DAO

A decentralized autonomous organization (DAO), also known as a decentralized autonomous corporation (DAC) is an ecosystem whose function is regulated by smart contracts (see Smart Contract for more information on this term.) Relevant examples of this type of organizations are the Dash governance and Digix.io.

In most countries, the DAOs are not fully regulated. Moreover, the legal status is ultimately unclear. The functionality of these ecosystems is based on the blockchain technology to keep a shared record of the transactions in the network. There are security measures to prevent forgery and malicious manipulation of the database.

Digital asset

A digital asset is any type of information in a binary format with a right to be used. Without this right, an active is not considered an *asset*. There are several types of digital assets, such as documents, motion pictures, and much more. Among the numerous possibilities, the cryptocurrencies also belong to this category.

Besides, there is the need for a digital asset management (DAM) to implement the hardware and software interaction for the optimal use of the assets, i.e. make transactions with cryptocurrencies. The digital assets also contain metadata, which enable the possibility of having a register of the information of interest in the ecosystem. The metadata increases the knowledge about the assets, which become more accessible and manageable.

Cryptocurrency wallets store the access keys which authorize the owners to make use of the tokens in the network. Inside a cryptocoin system, the metadata is stored with encryption to prevent malicious users from hacking the access.

Difficulty (mining)

The issue of new cryptocurrency tokens is regulated to avoid saturation in the coin ecosystem. A way to establish control in this process, known as mining, relies on adjusting the *difficulty* level of the algorithms involved in the computational procedures.

Commonly referred to as simply difficulty, this is a measure of how complicated the Mathematical problems to solve have become in the mining (see Mining for more information) of new blocks. Furthermore, the difficulty level depends on the hashing power that is active in the cryptocurrency network at a given moment.

In the case of the Bitcoin, this complexity has grown at an

exponential pace; see the chart below with the bitcoin difficulty in the past two years.

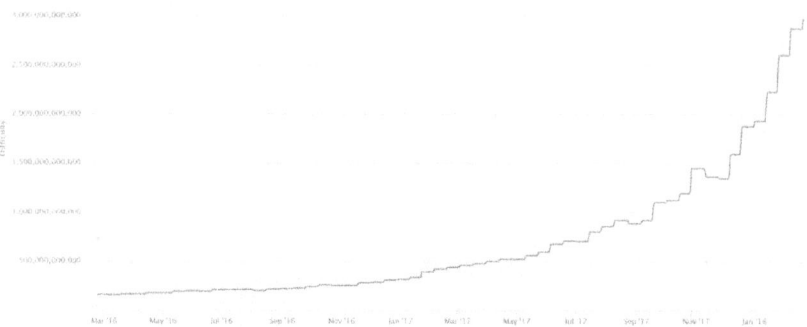

Source: https://blockchain.info/en/charts/difficulty?timespan=2 years

Fiat money / currency

Fiat is a type of currency which lacks intrinsic value *per se*. In the general case, it is the governments which regulate the value of a given issued currency. A government has a reputation for supporting a fiat currency, and to enforce the value or maintain the exchanging parties (other governments or entities) under an agreement about the worthiness of the money.

The fiat currencies can also be named *traditional* currencies, cash or just currencies to tell them apart from the cryptocoins. Thanks to the exchange services, fiat currencies, and cryptocoin tokens can be interchanged. There is a highly volatile component in the price of each cryptocurrency token in comparison to the stability of the fiat currencies depending on the influential factors.

The following chart shows the bitcoin price in a one-year scope.

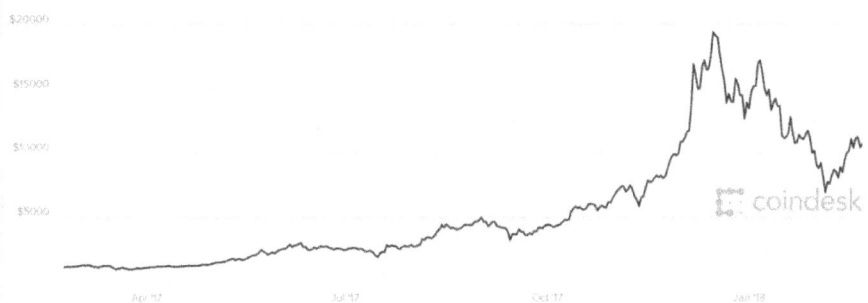

Source: https://www.coindesk.com/price/

On the other hand, the fluctuation of the USD value in the same period is of around 17% of its market value in relation to the euro (see the chart below). *Does it sound like a lot?*

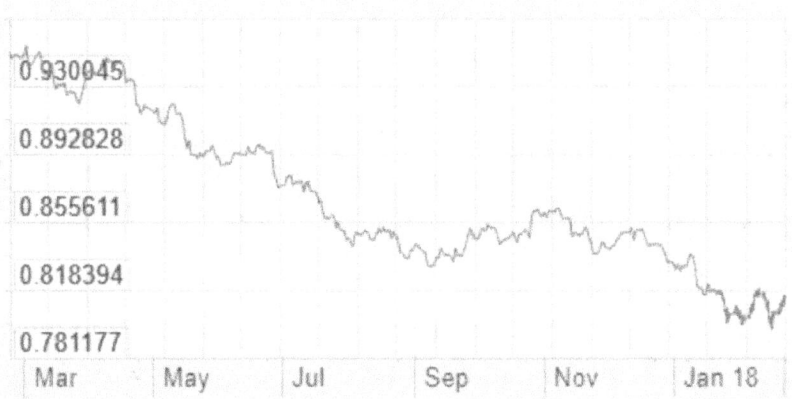

Source: www.x-rates.com

In the past year, the bitcoin token price has increased its value 1600% considering the historical extreme (min and max) market prices. Thus, cryptocurrencies are much more volatile than fiat currencies.

Mining

The process of issuing new cryptocurrency tokens is often called mining. Although it may sound a somewhat unrelated term for a computational method, it is very illustrative of the demands and limitation of the task.

Just like mining to find precious minerals, the issuing of cryptocurrency tokens takes up a great effort and plenty of time. Moreover, mining consumes resources, in the case of digital coins, computational power.

To get bitcoin tokens, you need to set a specific *computer* up for the job. In fact, the devices which offer profitability in Bitcoin mining are so powerful that are no longer regular computers; they are called ASICs (Check ASIC to learn more).

Ethereum mining demands GPU power, which is another case of resources dedicated to the token issuing. Most cryptocoins require a great deal of computational ability to reach the profitable zone, e.g. to have the positive benefit after the expenses, like the electricity bill.

There are also some cryptocurrencies which do not require mining, such as Ripple – whose max cap tokens already exist but are not entirely available for the users as of today (You can learn more about Ripple here).

Mining is one way of managing the ecosystem of a coin. On the bright side, it makes it unavoidable to flood the network with numerous tokens. However, mining requires a lot of dedication: computational power and time. The systems without mining save those expenses but need to elaborate alternative regulating mechanisms to have the economy under control.

Proof of Stake (POS)

The proof-of-stake algorithm is one of the procedures to achieve the distributed consensus that is required in the cryptocurrency ecosystem. Under the POS rules, the user responsible for generating the next block is selected randomly with the consideration of some status properties, such as the stake.

Although it has been proved that POS can be more energetically efficient than the POW-based algorithms, there has been criticism about this approach. Under POW mining, there is a chance for the miner not to own the token that the device assisted in creating. However, POS assigns the mining of the tokens to one user who will have the ownership guaranteed.

Detractors of POS as the means to achieve consensus in the network claim that the users without a stake may be able to profit from mining in multiple chains at the same time. Some studies have shown that such strategy could be profitable provided that the lower the stake, the fewer resources a user will need to dedicate to the mining.

The cryptocurrencies which base their mining in POS have searched for measures to handle the so-called *nothing-at-stake* problem. Plus, such users could vote in more than one chain to avoid consensus, which jeopardizes the normal function of the ecosystem. Ethereum and Peercoin have attempted different protocols to handle this flaw. There are also hybrid mining processes which combine the best of both algorithms, such as the Decred's mining.

Proof of Work (POW)

The proof-of-work system is a measure to avoid DoS (denial of service) attacks in the cryptocurrency network. Other malicious attempts, such as the spam or the manipulation of the consensus in the ecosystem are also prevented with POW algorithms.

The main premise of this asymmetric system consists of having a complex problem to solve by the requester while assuring simplicity in the checking on the provider's side. Bitcoin uses a POW function, like the Hashcash to track the transfers in the P2P network.

The difficulty of the mining procedures is adjusted periodically to keep the block time within a specific value. The power resources dedicated to this task in the Bitcoin network is one of the deciding factors for this tweak.

Each block contains the hash of the previous one. Therefore, the only way of changing a block in the ledger is by redoing the work of every previous work – which is not affordable computationally. In other words, the POW assures that the blockchain cannot be falsified.

Smart Contract

A smart contract allows the exchange of currency, property, shares, and assets of any kind under specific previously accepted terms. The main advantage of developing a platform that is compatible with smart contracts is that you can avoid having intermediaries.

Eliminating the middlemen in the contractual processes serves to reduce the costs. Plus, smart contracts introduce a transparent means of making transactions. A smart contract provides the digital counterpart of real-life paper contracts in the digital world. When the users comply with the conditions of the contract, the code is executed to make the corresponding transaction of assets.

The most outstanding advantage of the smart contracts is that the conditions are validated by hundreds of users of the network. For instance, if you want to rent an apartment paying with cryptocurrency, you'd need to send a given number of tokens before the mutually agreed date. Then, you should receive the keys to access the apartment also within a specific date. Otherwise, there would be a refund of the tokens.

The premise of the smart contract works under the if-then condition.

When the conditions are satisfied, the code executes the terms of the contract. Both parties can rest assure compliance with the terms thanks to the precision of the program which empower these contracts.

Source: Blockgeeks

The public ledger of the cryptocurrency network which is used to implement the smart contract helps in the validations of these terms. The Ethereum platform was the pioneer in this kind of interactions for the purchase of goods and services. Nowadays, there are several cryptocoins that have been developed to be fully compatible with smart contracts.

Token

Although in most cases the terms cryptocurrency and coin are often used interchangeably, there are differences worth noting. The alternative coins to the Bitcoin, namely altcoins, do not always have a currency system. Each bitcoin token stores value and counts on mediums of exchange, but that is not the case for every digital asset.

When a blockchain project is kickstarted, agreements and partnerships need to be secured to enable exchange services for fiat currencies. It is simpler to implement exchange among digital assets. The bitcoin was developed as a currency, but nowadays there are many tokens without feasibility to be changed for fiat money in a practical manner. Fortunately, you can always interchange tokens to get those with monetary value and listed in exchanges.

The most popular exchange services only host the top cryptocurrencies to be purchased with fiat money. For instance, Coinbase is compatible with four cryptocurrencies: Bitcoin, Bitcoin Cash, Ethereum, and Litecoin.

On the other side, services like Bittrex – arguably the exchange with more extensive token support – allows users to have wallets for almost 200 different tokens. There, you can exchange coins as you need and purchase cryptocurrencies whenever you want to get fiat money.

This image summarizes the different types of tokens and cryptocurrencies.

Cryptocurrency Masterclass 2018

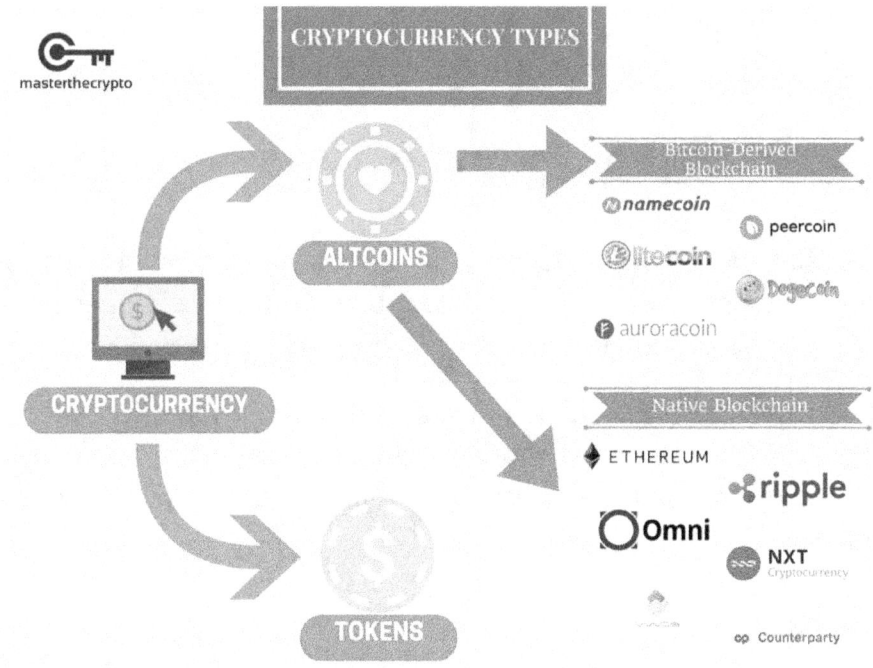

Source: Masterthecrypto.com

Setting up your bitcoin wallet

Now that you understand how the bitcoin system works, you are ready to create your first wallet. As I mentioned before, there are diverse types of wallets, according to the storing specs.

Below, we will review the major features of the wallets types, so you can decide which one is more suitable for your use. Later in this chapter, we will also discuss the security aspects of the wallets, protections tips and more.

Desktop wallets

The original bitcoin client, Bitcoin Core, allows users to have wallets in desktop (in the device they are using to run the client, which is often a computer). You can also create a wallet address to send and receive bitcoins.

The following are some of the most popular bitcoin desktop clients who also have mobile and web compatibility. In some cases, the wallet clients are available in the mainstream operative systems. Some even have mobile OS compatibility; which is always handy.

Airbitz

The world's first zero-knowledge single sign-on solution.

> **Official link:** https://airbitz.co/
>
> **Download link:** https://airbitz.co/app

Available for: iOS, Android

Target users: Everyone   **Multi-user:** Multi-wallet

Wallet security features: Encrypted, on-device and server backups.

Network security features: Partial

Backups: Automatic

Setup time: Instantaneous

Wallet maturity: Oct 2014

Armony

The only open-source wallet with cold storage and multi-signature support.

Official link: https://www.bitcoinarmory.com/

Download link: https://bitcoinarmory.com/download

Available for: iOS, Mac, Windows

Target users: Power users   **Multi-user:** Multi-wallet

Wallet security features: Encrypted and on-device

Network security features: Addon

Backups: One-time

Setup time: Hours

Wallet maturity: Jul 2011

Bitcoin Core

Helping everyone to keep the Bitcoin as a decentralized cryptocurrency.

Official link: https://bitcoin.org/en/bitcoin-core/
Download link: https://bitcoin.org/en/download
Available for: iOS, Mac, Windows
Target users: End-users   **Multi-user:** No
Wallet security features: Encrypted and on-device
Network security features: Full
Backups: Manual
Setup time: Hours
Wallet maturity: May 2011

Bitcoin Knots

Bitcoin Knots is a derivative of Bitcoin Core with some improvements and enhancements.

Official and download link: http://bitcoinknots.org/
Available for: iOS, Mac, Windows
Target users: End-users   **Multi-user:** Multi-wallet
Wallet security features: Encrypted and on-device
Network security features: Full
Backups: Manual

Setup time: Hours
Wallet maturity: Dec 2011

Bitcoind

Bitcoind is a program that implements the Bitcoin protocol for remote procedure call (RPC) use. It has been bundled with the original client (Bitcoin Core).

Official link: https://en.bitcoin.it/wiki/Bitcoind
Download link: https://bitcoin.org/en/download
Available for: iOS, Mac, Linux (ARM and Ubuntu), Windows
Target users: Programmers **Multi-user:** No
Wallet security features: Encrypted and on-device
Network security features: Full
Backups: Manual
Setup time: Hours
Wallet maturity: Aug 2009

Bitcoin Explorer (BX)

Bitcoin Explorer (BX) is an advanced command line application that is included as part of libbitcoin-explorer.

Official link: https://en.bitcoin.it/wiki/Bitcoin_Explorer
Available for: Linux, Mac, Windows
Target users: Power users **Multi-user:** Multi-wallet
Wallet security features: Ephemeral, Multisign Optional

Network security features: Full, with the local node
Backups: BIP39
Setup time: Instant
Wallet maturity: May 2011

Libbitcoin-explorer

A library with a console application to manage a wallet.

Official link: https://en.bitcoin.it/wiki/Libbitcoin_Explorer
Download link: https://github.com/libbitcoin/libbitcoin-explorer/wiki/Build-BX
Available for: Android, Linux, Mac, Windows
Target users: Programmers   **Multi-user:** Multi-wallet
Wallet security features: Ephemeral, Multisign Optional
Network security features: Full, with the local node
Backups: BIP39
Setup time: Instant
Wallet maturity: May 2011

Bitcoin Wallet

An open-source and free wallet implementation for the Android.

Official link: https://en.bitcoin.it/wiki/Bitcoin_Wallet
Download links: Android, Blackberry
Available for: Android, Blackberry
Target users: End-users   **Multi-user:** Compatible with JB tablets
Wallet security features: Isolated and on-device
Network security features: Partial
Backups: Manual
Setup time: Instant
Wallet maturity: Mar 2011

Blocktrail

Blocktrail is a Bitcoin wallet that puts you in full control of your Bitcoin. This wallet service has been acquired by BitMain.

Official link: https://www.blocktrail.com/
Download link: Android, iOS
Available for: Android and iOS
Target users: Everyone   **Multi-user:** No
Wallet security features: Encrypted, on-device, multisign, HD and backup server
Network security features: Remote
Backups: One-time

Setup time: Instant

Wallet maturity: Sep 2015

Electrum

Lightweight Bitcoin client, based on a client-server protocol.

Official link: https://electrum.org/#home

Download link: https://electrum.org/#download

Available for: Android, Linux, Mac, Windows

Target users: Power users   **Multi-user:** No

Wallet security features: Encrypted and on-device

Network security features: Minimal

Backups: Memorized

Setup time: Minutes

Wallet maturity: Nov 2011

Gocoin

An open-source Bitcoin wallet implementation solution that is written in Go language.

Official link: https://en.bitcoin.it/wiki/Gocoin

Build link: https://github.com/piotrnar/gocoin

Available for: Linux, Mac, Windows, FreeBSD

Target users: Power users   **Multi-user:** Multi-wallet

Wallet security features: Designated offline PC
Network security features: Full
Backups: Memorized
Setup time: Hours
Wallet maturity: May 2013

GreenAddress

Open source Bitcoin wallet client for both desktop and mobile.

Official link: https://en.bitcoin.it/wiki/GreenAddress
Download link: Web, Chrome, Android
Available for: Android, Linux, Mac, Windows
Target users: Everyone   **Multi-user:** Yes
Wallet security features: Encrypted and on-device
Network security features: Remote
Backups: Memorized and manual
Setup time: Instant
Wallet maturity: Apr 2013

MultiBit (no longer supported)

Lightweight, *thin client* Bitcoin multisystem wallet for Windows, MacOS, and Linux based on bitcoin – a client library built in Java. **This client is no longer supported. Further use is not**

recommended.

Official link: https://multibit.org/
Download link: https://multibit.org/releases.html
Available for: Linux, Mac, Windows
Target users: End-users   **Multi-user:** Multi-wallet
Wallet security features: Encrypted and on-device
Network security features: Partial
Backups: Automatic (local)
Setup time: Instant
Wallet maturity: Jul 2011

Mycelium

The Mycelium project has developed a number of Bitcoin-related products, such as payment gateways, local trading, and ATMs services.

Official link: https://wallet.mycelium.com/index.html
Download link: Android
Available for: iOS and Android
Target users: Everyone   **Multi-user:** No
Wallet security features: Isolated and on-device
Network security features: Partial
Backups: Manual and encrypted
Setup time: Instant

Wallet maturity: Sep 2013

My Wallet

A web-based wallet client to make transactions with bitcoin tokens.

Official link: https://blockchain.info/wallet/#/signup

Available for: Android, iOS, Mac, Linux, Windows

Target users: Everyone   **Multi-user:** Yes

Wallet security features: Encrypted and on-server

Network security features: Remote

Backups: Automatic

Setup time: Minutes

Wallet maturity: Dec 2011

Mobile wallets

A mobile wallet stores the payment card information in a handy device, such a Smartphone or a tablet. The main advantage of a mobile wallet is the possibility of making in-store purchases with merchants listed in the compatible mobile service provider's platform.

The main purpose of a Bitcoin wallet is to send and receive tokens. Furthermore, the wallet client should enforce security measures to avoid malicious attempts to grab the BTC stored on the device. For instance, double confirmations, biometric scans, and the like serve to ensure the high-standard security that is required.

Among the most reliable and supported bitcoin mobile wallets, there are the following:

- **Mycelium.** This wallet has advanced privacy and security features. Although this wallet does not have web or desktop versions, it is one of the safest out there. Plus, this mobile wallet is regularly updated and has compatibility with a hardware wallet to enhance the security of your precious tokens. This wallet is not new-user-friendly; it has plenty of features.

  Mycelium official website. Compatible with Android and iOS.

- **BreadWallet.** If you prefer simplicity, then this wallet is your bread and butter. The only features are the Send and Receive options. On the downside, there are no enhanced security features to protect your tokens. Thus, it's better not to store large amounts of tokens in this wallet.

  BreadWallet official website. Compatible with Android and iOS.

- **Copay.** The wallet created by BitPay (a well-known cryptocurrency exchange) enables multisignature[3] as an enhanced security feature. Although this feature improves the security, it may turn transactions to be slower than otherwise.

  CoPay official website. Multiplatform.

- **Jaxx.** Arguably the most intuitive and versatile mobile wallet out there. However, this client is not open source, and a safety concern has not been solved since August 2017 as of February

---

[3] This feature enforces a given number of users in the network to approve a transaction to validate the change of ownership of the tokens.

2018: the 12-word backup phrase can be extracted from local storage in any implementation of this wallet.

Thus, it is recommended to use this wallet carefully or to avoid the regular use until this security flaw is solved.

> Jaxx official website. Download (iOS, Android, Chrome, and Windows)

- **AirBitz.** This wallet can be as user-friendly as BreadWallet, but the client has more advanced features. For instance, you can purchase gift cards for a number of merchants with the use of this wallet.

> AirBitz official website. Download site (iOS and Android)

- **GreenAddress or GreenBits.** When you get some experience with the use of Bitcoin, you can try this wallet. Although this wallet is a bit more challenging to use, the security and features are worth the try.

> GreenBits official website. Compatible with Android.

Note: Do not confuse exchanges with wallets. Usually, wallets allow cryptocurrency transactions, and possibly some enhanced features. On the other side, the exchanges are focused on cryptocurrency tokens purchase and interchange with fiat currency. For instance, Coinbase is a popular exchange service which has in-app wallets.

You should always:

- Set a pin for protection for your wallet or an alternative security method, such as a biometric measure (fingerprint scan).

- Avoid storage of large amounts of tokens in a mobile wallet.

- Have the 12 or 24-word backup phrase written down and kept safe. That sequence of random words in a correlated order will let you restore your wallet.

Online wallets

In general, the online cryptocurrency wallets are not the safest. Most of the online clients have implemented means to enhance the security, such as double verifications or PIN codes. However, if you want the ultimate protection, you should opt for a hardware wallet instead, such as Trezor, Ledger Nano, or others.

GreenAddress is one of the most versatile wallets, which is also supported in other environments. StrongCoin is probably the most protected online wallet – with complete encryption of the backup passphrase. Keep in mind that storing a large number of tokens in an online wallet is not a recommended practice.

Exchange services

An exchange is a token interchange provider which allows cryptocurrency to fiat money transactions and vice-versa. You can buy and sell bitcoin tokens, or trade with the supported altcoins in the exchange. Moreover, there could be additional services to empower the use of the service provider.

Coinbase

One of the most well-established exchanges worldwide. Coinbase supports four of the top cryptocoins in the market, namely Bitcoin, Bitcoin Cash, Litecoin, and Ethereum. Setting up your account in this service is quite straightforward, you can start receiving tokens within minutes.

However, to make buy or sell tokens with fiat currency, you will need to verify at least one payment method. Coinbase supports credit cards and fiat transfers to fund the cryptocurrency tokens purchases. You can have tokens stored in the supported wallets and generate new addresses for safe transactions.

Coinbase is available in web and mobile - secured with a 4-digit PIN code. You can also enable the two-step verification for further precaution to get an SMS code which verifies your identity.

Bittrex

If you want to have wallets for several cryptocurrencies without having to install clients on your PC, Bittrex is the way to go. This exchange has a large number of cryptocoins to trade: +190 different tokens. This exchange has a very acceptable withdraw timing and a reliable order execution – so, you will not be getting error messages when you send or receive coins.

There are several exchanges out there which you can try with precaution. Depending on the country you are based, you may be interested in some of them rather than others. This is a short list highlighting the most famous ones:

Exchange	Country	Currency	Rating + Opinion
eToro	UK	USD	High, user-friendly
CryptoGo	UK	All fiat	Outstanding, cards accepted
Binance	China	Cryptocurrency	Cardano, NEM accepted

24 option	Local	All currencies	Cards and bank transfers
LocalBitcoins	Local	All currencies	Cards and transfers
Coinbase	USA	USA, GBP, EUR	Cards and transfers
Cex.io	UK	USD, GBP, EUR, RUB	Cards, transfers, and ETH
Xcoins	USA	USD, EUR, GBP	Cards, transfers, and Paypal
Changelly	CZ	Cryptocurrency and credit cards	Highly rated
Paxful	USA	Paypal, debit card, Neteller, Skrill, Amazon, iTunes, etc.	9.20 / 10
Coinmama	Slovakia	USD, EUR, ETH, BTC	Cards and bank transfers
Kraken	USA	USD, EUR, CAD, GBP, JPY	Bank transfers and altcoins
Poloniex	USA	+172 cryptocoins	Cryptocurrency
Gemini	USA	Bank transfers	Highly rated
Blockchain	LX	EUR	Cards accepted
CoinExchange.io	Not regulated	+190 cryptocurrencies	Cryptocurrency accepted only
Bitcoin.de	Germany	EUR	Bank transfers accepted

Bithumb	South Korea	+8 cryptocurrencies	Cards and bank transfers
CoinATMRadar	World ATM map	All currencies	Cash only

There are many other exchanges out there; you can check a top 44 list here. Keep in mind that it is not advisable to store a large number of tokens in exchange, you should rely on a hardware wallet for that purpose instead. Moreover, you should make small transactions to test the transaction responses of the system and know if the features are up to your needs.

Hardware wallets

This type of wallets stores the user's private keys in a more secure environment, an offline hardware device. A hardware wallet is the ultimate means to secure your precious tokens. You will only need to move your tokens to the device to have them in an inaccessible vault.

Literally, the only way to get a hand on those tokens is to steal the hardware device. And even then, the malicious stealer should know your PIN code or authentication method to have access to the private keys. There is no way to have remote access to a device that is not connected to the internet.

These are the top reasons why you should consider getting a hardware wallet to secure tokens:

- The private keys are stored in a protected area of the microcontroller. The keys cannot be extracted as plain text.
- Cannot be affected by any computer virus.

- A hardware wallet is interactive.

- Most hardware wallets are open source.

Paper wallets

Memory wallets

Basic bitcoin trading ideas

As in the stock market, the central premise to earn dividends with cryptocurrencies is to sell higher than you buy. However, it can be a challenge to do so in such a volatile market. As you can see in the chart below, the price is always fluctuating. Therefore, you'll need to be wary about when to buy or sell in order to get profit.

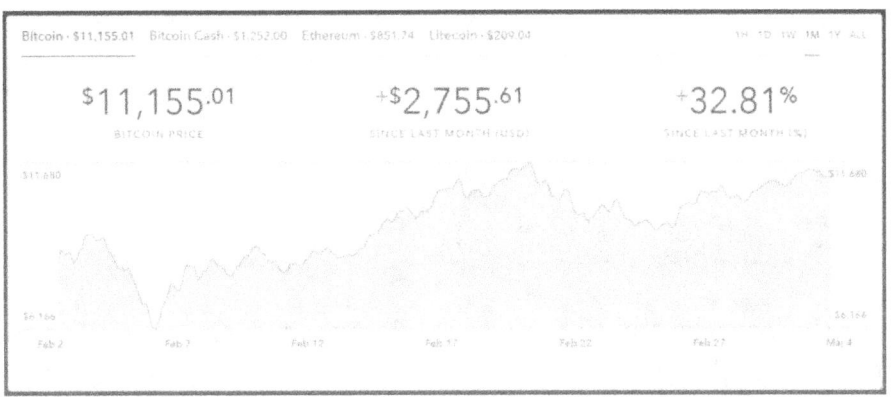

On one side, betting on the strongest cryptocurrency is the best way to go. In other words, BTC or ETH have stayed in the top of the wave of this new market for months. Thus, it is not expected to see their market capitalization decrease drastically. It is still possible that the per-token price goes down or up considerably.

For instance, in early February 2018, the price of the bitcoin went as down as USD7,000. Right now, one month later, the token price for this cryptocurrency has escalated back to USD11,000 and seems to follow an upward trend. As a conclusion, we could say that it is only a matter of time until the bitcoin prices go back to where it has been hovering for weeks.

Buy or sell?

Of course, nobody knows when – if ever – the bitcoin price will ramp up to the USD20,000 milestone that occurred in December 2017. Right now, even after the recovery of early 2018, the price is only 50% of that historical record. You should not bet all your chances to that event ever taking place again.

In the long run, it could or could not happen. Such records occur occasionally. And, thus, are called records for a reason. In any case, we can understand how the token prices changes in the one-year view.

After the exponential growth of the last quarter of 2017, we had a downside tendency which seems to be over. The chances are that the price for this cryptocurrency will remain high in 2018. That is the most likely outcome for the strongest cryptocoins.

As a rule, I do not recommend purchasing cryptocurrency – it is better to sell the tokens when the right time shows up only. **How can you obtain the tokens in the first place, then?** You can exchange service, a product or get a tip in the form of cryptocurrencies.

Why not make use of fiat to purchase BTC or any other crypto? Imagine that you buy the tokens that correspond to 1,000USD today and that the price of the BTC goes down USD400 tomorrow. You'd have lost 40% of your investment overnight.

That's too hard of a hit for anyone stepping into the cryptocurrency world, but it can happen. Maybe, within a week you could recover the worth of the tokens, or it could take a month. Nobody knows for sure. **Is that worth your initial inversion?** I think not.

In the other case scenario, you provide a service or sell an item accepting BTC token as payment. Imagine that you have a service/product which is worth USD50, but you charge USD75 in BTC tokens to account for fluctuations. **What happens now in the case that the token price sinks 40% overnight?** You would only "lose" USD30, i.e. you'd still have USD45 in BTC tokens! – which is basically the original price of the item or service, by the way. Thus, by inflating your revenue by 50%, you are covered for fluctuations of around 40%, doesn't it sound good enough? But wait, you could still earn money if the token price went up instead. **What would happen if the BTC tokens would be valued 40% more the next day?** In that case, you'd have USD105 in BTC – i.e. no less than USD30 of extra revenue by doing nothing yourself!

As I see it, banking cryptocoins in exchange for services or products is the way to go. Most people will accept the extra fees that come along with the payment method. After all, cryptocurrencies are volatile; they are not valued a constant amount of fiat currency to worry for a bit higher price.

Last, there are also tips which you can get on various websites, such as SteemIt and others. Read this post to know more about those services. Getting some tips is an easy way to get a stake of cryptocoins, only by contributing to the community. Exchange your knowledge about the BTC with the world; people will thank you for some tokens.

When the price goes to the roof, it's time to sell those tokens!

Alternative cryptocurrencies: The Altcoins

Once the bitcoin hype spread, developers from all over the world started projects to create different versions of the original cryptocurrency. The "alternative coins", in short Altcoins, are the cryptocurrencies which share the core source code of the bitcoin but differ in other features.

What differentiates the Altcoins from the bitcoin?

Among the various features, there are the following:

- They have their own blockchain.
- They have their P2P (peer-to-peer) network.
- They may have a different mining process.
- They may implement POW (Proof of Work) or POS (Proof of Stake) algorithms.
- They could have more than one operative network to make it possible to enable more advanced features.

We will review the pros and cons of the top cryptocurrency projects to understand the differences in more detail. In short, the aim of these Altcoins is to provide innovations that go beyond the bitcoin network to this growing market, such as instant payments for instance.

The failure or success of the Altcoins projects depends on various factors, such as popularity, utility, usability, etc. However, we could agree that the top 20 are by far the most successful crypto assets as of today. Plus, these tokens are more likely to stay in a dominant position in the future.

There are thousands of cryptocoins in the global market, but most of them are not interchangeable for fiat currency – at least, not in a practical manner. The young projects aim to have tokens that are compatible (tradeable) with already-existing one.

In any case, a token holder can always purchase some of the top cryptocurrencies in a previous step before using an exchange to get fiat money. Then, it's just a matter of withdrawing the fiat to your bank account.

Each of the cryptocurrencies which came after the Bitcoin is often called altcoin. Therefore, the term is widely used regardless of the market capitalization.

Top 20 cryptocurrencies in the market

Please, note that the list on *Coinmarketcap* may have changed by the time you read this book. The above-listed cryptocurrencies are some of the strongest in the market in any case and should be considered as a reliable reference.

The following list serves as a short summary of the main features of the top 20 cryptocoins according to market capitalization. In other words, these are the digital assets whose tokens maintain the highest amount of value in fiat currencies.

#1 Bitcoin: the original cryptocoin

The first cryptocurrency and a worldwide decentralized payment system based on peer-to-peer transactions without a third party's participation, based on a distributed ledger called the blockchain.

Logo:

Symbol: ☐ (Widely accepted) Other: B, B, ฿ (Thai Baht).

Currency code / Ticker symbol: BTC (most popular), XBT (official)

Year of release: 2009

Websites: https://bitcoin.org/, https://bitcoin.com/

Market capitalization (Feb 2018): $183.540 billion

Mined Tokens (Feb 2018): 16.8 million BTC

Maximum Supply: 21 million BTC
Source on Coinmarketcap: https://coinmarketcap.com/currencies/bitcoin/

A short story of the Bitcoin

Bitcoin succeeded where others failed. The previous attempts at creating encrypted currencies with ledgers, such as B-Money or Bit gold, did not pass the formulation stage. In 2008, a paper submitted by mailing list forever changed the way we understand currency.

The only regret is that we do not know who to thank for the initial development of the bitcoin. The author – or authors – of the paper called Bitcoin – A peer to peer Electronic Cash System signed as Satoshi Nakamoto.

However, nobody knows who this person or team is. The mysterious origins of the bitcoin serve to further enhance the legend. In just 9 pages, the paper describes the basics of the digital cash system and hints on how to introduce a mechanism to avoid double spends.

In 2009, the first Bitcoin client was released to the public so that the users could mine their own tokens and contribute to the network. It was not until 2010 that someone used the mined tokens to make a purchase, two pizzas at the price of 10.000 tokens.

Today, those tokens would be worth over $100 million. Arguably the most expensive pizzas of all times as of today's standards. Other cryptocurrencies were developed as the popularity of the bitcoin increased. The era of the digital currencies started, but it was just the beginning.

In 2013, the price of the bitcoin crashed dramatically. Just after reaching the $1.000 per token price for the first time, the market value decreased rapidly to around $300. It was not until 2015 when the price ramped up to the previous values.

One of the worldwide largest bitcoin exchange suffered a historical attack in 2014. 850.000 bitcoin tokens went missing after a disruption of Mt. Gox exchange service caused by a malicious attack. Those tokens were worth $450 million back then, and nowadays their price is estimated at $4.4 billion.

The ICOs kicked in during 2016. The arrival of the ICOs was also marked by the development of a rival cryptocurrency, the Ether on the Ethereum platform. The central premise of the alternative cryptocoin, the second one in the market capitalization rank, is to enable the creation of smart contracts and app based on the blockchain.

In 2017, the cryptocurrency market expanded beyond the most optimistic forecasts. The bitcoin surpassed the $20.000 per token price in the exchanges. The cryptocoin market has been growing rapidly and relentlessly. There thousands of altcoins out there and more being developed right now.

Although the price of the bitcoin decreased notably by the end of 2017, it has shown signs of recovery. Some days after reaching the lowest price of $6.000 per token in January 2018, 1 BTC was worth around $12.000 by the first fortnight of February 2018. The tendency shows a growing trend in the market price.

Some experts claim that the bitcoin and the altcoins are the future of digital monetary transactions. Detractors state that the bitcoin is a colossal scam based on Ponzi schemes, and so are the ICOs. Obviously, we cannot neglect that some malicious groups have carried out frauds.

Moreover, the cryptocurrencies have been widely used by illegal sectors worldwide due to the anonymity of the transactions. In any case, the criminal activities can also be funded with fiat currencies. The bitcoin is here to stay for a long time regardless the controversy and the lack of regulation in most countries – which will eventually occur.

#2 Ethereum

Ether is the cryptocurrency that fuels the distributed application platform Ethereum is the form of payment by the clients for the services in the network. Ethereum and Ether are often interchangeable in the cryptocurrency context.

Logo:

Symbol: Ξ (Not widely used). Some users propose the symbol based on the Ethereum project logo: ♦

Currency code / Ticker symbol: ETH

Year of release: 2015

Website: https://www.ethereum.org/

Market capitalization (Feb 2018): $93.242 million

Mined Tokens (Feb 2018): 97.7 million ETH

Maximum Supply: 97.7 million ETH

Source on Coinmarketcap: https://coinmarketcap.com/currencies/ethereum/

A short story of Ethereum

The creation of Ethereum is linked to the development of the smart contracts. Two types of account can be created in the ETH ecosystem: the human-owned accounts and the contract accounts. This feature allows developers to create any kind of decentralized application based on the blockchain technology.

Although Ethereum was developed based on the bitcoin, there are some fundamental differences between both cryptocurrencies:

- Ethereum allows transactions with the platform's cryptocurrency Ether, smart contracts and Ethereum Virtual Machine (EVM). Bitcoin only allows transactions with cryptocurrency.

- ETH works with POS whereas Bitcoin operates with POW.

- Ethereum allows permissioned (only a restricted number of users can contribute to the consensus of the network) and permissionless (any user can join and start mining tokens) transactions. Bitcoin operates in a permissionless environment.

- The average block time is much lower in ETH than in Bitcoin, e.g. 12 seconds opposed to 10 minutes, respectively. Therefore, Ethereum improves the response time of the network allowing users to mine more tokens in given amount of time.

- There are more ETH tokens than BTC tokens. Issuance of ether is capped at 18 million tokens per year. On its side, there is a 21 million bitcoin tokens cap, out of which almost 17 million have already been mined.

In short, Ethereum offers more possibilities than just cryptocurrency transaction. Companies like JPMorgan Chase, Intel and Microsoft have already invested in this cryptocurrency. Some experts have forecast that ETH will eventually dominate the market.

Although we cannot tell if this switch of predominance will occur, it is evident that Ethereum and Bitcoin have by far the highest market capitalizations in the cryptocurrency market. Ethereum has remained in the rank #2 for a long time.

The key differentiator of Ethereum is the capability of transacting more than just cryptocurrency. Vitalik Buterin, Ethereum's co-founder, envisioned a different approach to cover more functionalities than the bitcoin network.

Recently, there have been forks in the Ethereum blockchain, which led to the development of Ethereum Classic (ETC), Expanse (EXP), Ethereum Fog (ETF), and EtherZero (ETZ). Ethereum Classic is the most successful project among the forks, which is currently in the top 20 cryptocurrencies according to market capitalization.

Despite the short story of this platform and the price fluctuations, Ethereum has grown drastically during the past months. In the long run, this ecosystem is looking for the ultimate solution in the cryptocurrency market. However, only time will show us which leading project will dominate.

We are still waiting for the reforms that bitcoin will undertake. In that front, Ethereum is already well-suited for the task. Inherently an adaptive a more versatile network, ETH will keep attracting investors despite the usual unavoidable of the cryptocoin market.

#3 Ripple

The Ripple transaction protocol (RTXP) or directly Ripple protocol is the currency exchange and remittance network created by the homonymous company. Ripple enables instant and nearly charge-free secure transactions. XRP is popular in the banking sector.

Logo: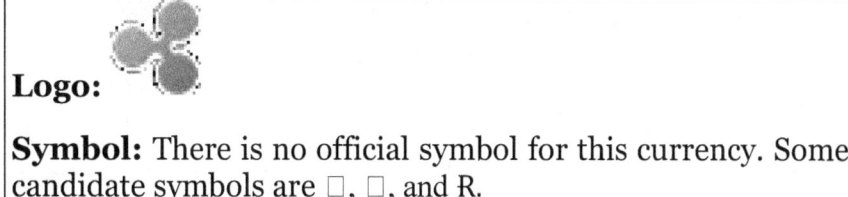

Symbol: There is no official symbol for this currency. Some candidate symbols are □, □, and R.

> **Currency code / Ticker symbol:** XRP
>
> **Year of release:** 2013
>
> **Website:** https://ripple.com/
>
> **Market capitalization (Feb 2018):** $44.529 million
>
> **Available Tokens (Feb 2018):** 39.009 million XRP
>
> **Maximum Supply:** 100.000 million XRP
>
> **Source on Coinmarketcap:** https://coinmarketcap.com/currencies/ripple/

A short story of Ripple

Ripple was developed as an alternative to wire transfers. Due to cross-currency settlements, one of such transactions may take several days to complete. The interledger protocol of Ripple handles transactions between one bank's ledged with that another bank. The transactions are complete with the use of XRP tokens.

The low price of the tokens (currently around $1 in February 2018) attracts plenty of users. On the one side, there is a little investment needed to get started. But, on the brighter side, the price has been fluctuating to even triple the current market value. Imaging investing $100 today and getting $200 or $300 in some weeks?

That could be possible with Ripple if the prices ramp up back to those the historical record of January 8th, 2018. The massive number of XRP tokens is the main reason behind the low price since the total supply is of 100.000 million XRP. Therefore, there is yet a lot of mining to do for this cryptocurrency.

On top of the mining feasibility, there are banking partners contributing to the development of the Ripple project. The international interest in this cryptocoin forecasts a promising future.

#4 Bitcoin Cash

The most important fork of the bitcoin blockchain which is getting a lot of support in the worldwide community.

> **Logo:**
>
> **Symbol:** No official symbol for this cryptocurrency.
>
> **Currency code / Ticker symbol:** BCH (official) and BCC (in some exchanges).
>
> **Year of release:** 2017
>
> **Websites:** https://www.bitcoincash.org/
>
> **Market capitalization (Feb 2018):** $25.833 million
>
> **Mined Tokens (Feb 2018):** 16.9 million BCH
>
> **Maximum Supply:** 21 million BCH
>
> **Source on Coinmarketcap:** https://coinmarketcap.com/currencies/bitcoin-cash/

A short story of Bitcoin Cash

During the first semester of 2017, it was announced that an upcoming hard fork of the bitcoin blockchain would occur. In August 2017, the fork took place, allowing users to start trading with the new cryptocurrency: Bitcoin Cash was born.

BCH was developed as an alternative to the popular use of the bitcoin. Back in May 2017, some users suffered for days to have their transactions confirmed. Days! Can you imagine that?

Think of going to a cafeteria and ordering a cup of coffee. Then, you make the payment, but there is an unexpected reply from the barista:

"You have to wait four days to have this transaction confirmed. Only then, you can come to pick your coffee." We'll keep it hot. – he may add.

On top of that, transaction fees were becoming prohibitive for small operations. Coming back to the cafeteria example, imagine that the barista says: "And, do not forget the transaction fee of $15 for the $3 cup of coffee." Complete madness, right?

Well, it's easy to understand why many users of Bitcoin were on their nerves in those weeks. Thus, the fork aimed to include improvements to handle such limitations. Right now, the only way developers can introduce software updates to the Bitcoin network. As a fact, both split blockchains are identical up to the point when the fork occurred.

From that moment, BTC and BCH are independent. Moreover, those who held bitcoin tokens at the instant of the fork were also given BCH tokens. The new cryptocurrency introduced lower fees and quicker transactions for the users. Hence, BCH provides a more versatile ecosystem.

Due to the prolonged debate about increasing the block size limit in the bitcoin environment, the initiative of having a fork was considered as the best approach. Bitcoin generally adopted SegWit in 2017 to reduce the transaction fees. Although some top exchanges are yet to follow that path, the strategy seems to have succeeded.

The 1MB block size limit in the Bitcoin network was causing the delays in the service. BCH raised the block size limit to 8MB to account for more transactions in less time. Moreover, SegWit will not be adopted in Bitcoin Cash in the foreseeable future.

Coming from the first cryptocurrency, BCH has proved to be a relevant alternative. Although this digital asset has not been around for too long, it has been in the top 5 according to market capitalization since the first day. Therefore, it's not surprising that this token has so many followers.

Some users believe that BCH has solved all the issues of the BTC. Is this cryptocoin the ultimate solution for digital transactions? There is no way to knowing for sure, but one thing is clear: BCH has come to stay. Plus, there are way more transactions per second in the Bitcoin Cash network than there are with BTC.

The BCH price peaked at around $4.000 per token in early December 2017. Since then, the market value followed the same recession than the bitcoin. Although they are independent assets, they belong to the same market. Hence, the factors which lowered the price of the BTC at the beginning of 2018 also affected the BCH.

As of February 2018, the token value is of $1.500 for each BCH token. And, there is currently a growing value tendency in the crypto market.

#5 Litecoin

As its name verses, this cryptocurrency was developed to be light. The 2.5 min block processing time is 4 times faster than in the bitcoin network. Faster, smarter and cheaper. Let there be lite!

Logo:

Symbol: Ł

Currency code / Ticker symbol: LTC

Year of release: 2011

Websites: https://litecoin.com/, https://litecoin.org/

Market capitalization (Feb 2018): $12.617 million

> **Mined Tokens (Feb 2018):** 55.2 million LTC
>
> **Maximum Supply:** 84 million LTC
>
> **Source on Coinmarketcap:**
> https://coinmarketcap.com/currencies/litecoin/

A short story of Litecoin

The faster block processing time is just the icing on the cake. Litecoin allows a lot more token than the bitcoin, up to 84 million. Moreover, the mining process is more distributed than in the case of the BTC. Finally, LTC was the first cryptocurrency to enable SegWit to improve the processing speed and lower transaction fees.

Litecoin will serve different purchasing purposes than Bitcoin. For instance, LTC could be used for small and quick transactions, such as everyday purchases. On the other hand, the bitcoin is a better option to make larger purchases due the longer processing times.

Compared to the bitcoin's SHA-256 hashing algorithm, the mining algorithm (Script) is more straightforward in the case of LTC. This means that users can mine these tokens with less powerful devices in comparison to the case of the bitcoin. Considering how prohibitive the cost of ASICs has become for bitcoin mining, this feature is a plus for LTC.

To understand the transactions times in perspective, let us consider that one confirmation may take 10 minutes with bitcoin. However, you can get two confirmations within 5 minutes in the LTC network. As most exchanges demand a minimum of 6 endorsements to validate transactions, it is usual to require one hour or more to have an operation confirmed with BTC. You'd need 15 min with Litecoin.

#6 Cardano

Cardano in a platform to manage smart contracts, apps, chains, computation, and metadata. The transactions are paid with its own cryptocurrency, ADA.

Logo:
Symbol: A
Currency code / Ticker symbol: ADA
Year of release: 2017
Websites: https://www.cardanohub.org/
Market capitalization (Feb 2018): $10.222 million
Mined Tokens (Feb 2018): 25.927 million ADA
Maximum Supply: 45.000 million ADA
Source on Coinmarketcap: https://coinmarketcap.com/currencies/cardano/

A short story of Cardano

The ADA cryptocurrency is rather recent, although the project started in 2015. There are several design premises which guided the development of the Cardano platform. This venture did not begin with a clear roadmap or a whitepaper.

The most outstanding features behind the design of this environment include:

- An accounting and a computation layer.

- Core components in a modular functional code.

- Development of decentralized funding capabilities.
- Exploration of the social features of the e-commerce.
- Interdisciplinary dev and research teams with InfoSec experts.

ADA is not unrelated to the long POW vs POS debate. The developers opted for the proof of stake for the Cardano platform because it has more scalability potential and versatility. Cardano is the first blockchain environment to evolve out of a scientific approach.

The open source and patent-free spirit conduct the way of ADA.

The designers of Cardano claim that their development is the more precisely engineered cryptocurrency. For instance, updates can be introduced by soft forks in this blockchain.

#7 NEO

Initially launched in 2014 by the name of AntShares, this Chinese cryptocurrency can process 10.000 transactions per second. This cryptocurrency co-exists with another asset in its network, GAS.

Logo:

Symbol: No official symbol yet.

Currency code / Ticker symbol: NEO

Year of release: 2016

Websites: https://neo.org/

Market capitalization (Feb 2018): $8.458 million

Mined Tokens (Feb 2018): 65 million NEO

> **Maximum Supply:** 100 million NEO
>
> **Source on Coinmarketcap:**
> https://coinmarketcap.com/currencies/neo/

A short story of NEO

NEO has similar aims than the Ethereum project. This cryptocurrency environment has some advanced features worth to highlight, such as:

- A consensus mechanism for Delegated Byzantine Fault Tolerance (DBFT).

- Operations across multiple blockchains, NeoX.

- The possibility of creating smart contracts, with NEO Contract.

- A decentralized storage service, NeoFS, like a P2P "Dropbox".

- NeoQ: a quantum-proof extra security encrypted layer.

Plus, we should note these are these pros of the NEO environment:

- NEO is compatible with the corporative use of applications.

- NEO can be used for currency and for programming with most of the programming languages.

- No need for mining with this cryptocurrency.

- NEO doesn't offer complete anonymity. Illegal activities can be tracked with this digital asset.

- NEO links digital and physical assets.

Users pay for smart contracts in GAS, depending on the computing resources needed. The contributors get tokens as a reward for their service. This 2-token ecosystem is complex but undoubtedly useful.

#8 Stellar

Another successful cryptocurrency platform which has kicked in with its own asset, the lumens. Let us review its strengths.

Logo:

Symbol: No official symbol for this cryptocurrency yet.

Currency code / Ticker symbol: XLM (Previously, STR)

Year of release: 2014

Websites: https://www.stellar.org/

Market capitalization (Feb 2018): $8.444 million

Mined Tokens (Feb 2018): 18.467 million XLM

Maximum Supply: 103.708 million XLM

Source on Coinmarketcap: https://coinmarketcap.com/currencies/stellar/

A short story of Stellar

Stellar is a distributed hybrid blockchain which allows transactions of small amounts, even fractions of a cent. In this regard, the use of Lumens goes one step ahead than Bitcoin. Stellar makes it possible to make quick transactions that would not be feasible with other cryptocurrencies due to prohibitive transactions fees.

The servers of this network keep in sync and store identical ledgers with the records of the accounts. Every 2 or 4 seconds, the servers update the status of all the accounts to reach an agreement due to consensus. The transactions are proposed to the ledgers by changing an account balance or a property of an account.

The Stellar developments have drawn the attention of nonprofits and businesses. Partnerships have been announced worldwide based on Stellar. Funded with Lumens as the interchangeable token, there are messaging apps, banking software tools, and more.

The future of XLM is optimistic. Making micropayments possible is just one advantage of using this platform. This payment system is meant to connect banks, apps, people and reduce the cost of transactions at nearly no cost per operation.

Stellar provides mobile branches and allows services for the underbanked. A feasible way to start micro savings with low-cost accounts is possible with XLM.

#9 EOS

A platform to support and develop industrial decentralized applications. EOS blockchain aims to eventually remove transaction fees and allow a vast amount of operations per second.

Logo:

Symbol: No official symbol for this cryptocurrency.

Currency code / Ticker symbol: EOS

Year of release: 2017

Website: https://eos.io/

Market capitalization (Feb 2018): $6.582 million

> **Mined Tokens (Feb 2018):** 678 million EOS
>
> **Maximum Supply:** 1.000 million EOS
>
> **Source on Coinmarketcap:**
> https://coinmarketcap.com/currencies/eos/

A short story of EOS

EOS was developed to offer decentralized hosting, smart contract compatibility, and storage for corporative uses. The scalability issues that the bitcoin and other cryptocurrency ecosystems suffer have been solved with this development.

Among the advanced features that EOS has, we should highlight the multithread (simultaneous use of computer cores) and the delegated proof of stake to enable the consensus protocol. In fact, EOS provides a fully decentralized operative system where multiple apps run with a proportional use of resources according to the owned tokens.

For instance, if someone had the 1% of the EOS available tokens at a given moment, this user could make use of the 1% of the total computational power of the network. Plus, the token owners can vote to decide about the network governance. This system has proved to be an effective way of decentralized autonomous organization (DAO) where the collective depends on the tokens stake of each user.

It is also worth to mention that the block processing time is as short as 500ms. Compared to other cryptocurrencies, EOS operates incredibly fast. This DAO scheme hosts apps on the platform which could not be censored by a given country's government due to the autonomy of its functionalities.

#10 IOTA

The new distributed ledger technology which aims to be the backbone of the Internet of Things is IOTA. This ecosystem is scalable, quantum-proof, and highly applicable to use cases.

> **Logo:**
>
> **Symbol:** No official symbol, but some users propose Ɨ, i or *i*.
>
> **Currency code / Ticker symbol:** MIOTA
>
> **Year of release:** 2017
>
> **Website:** https://iota.org/
>
> **Market capitalization (Feb 2018):** $5.773 million
>
> **Mined Tokens (Feb 2018):** 2.779 million MIOTA
>
> **Maximum Supply:** 2.779 million MIOTA
>
> **Source on Coinmarketcap:** https://coinmarketcap.com/currencies/iota/

A short story of IOTA

IOTA changed the conception of cryptocurrency. There is no mining, no blocks, and no transaction fees with this ecosystem. To validate a personal transaction, each user must previously help in the validation of two external transactions in the network. This proof of work scheme allows the absence of transactions fees or mining centralization.

In other words, the users with more computational power do not have bandwidth priority while using this digital asset. This P2P net is aiming to the IoT, providing data integrity and industrial uses, such as pay on demand, micropayments, sensor technology, etc.

Furthermore, IOTA is aiming to be usable in the future, where thousands of transactions will be required in the blockchains. Thus, Bitcoin and other cryptocurrencies are not yet suited for the exponential demand. Moreover, the existence of fees in those networks does not make it possible to perform microtransactions.

This payment system is not based on the blockchain, but on a directed acyclic graph (DAG), also known as the Tangle. All the MIOTA tokens were distributed among the shareholders since the initial release. Since there is no mining, the computational demands are lower than those in the blockchain-based environments.

In this section, we review the next ten digital assets according to market capitalization.

#11 Dash

Formerly known as Darkcoin and Xcoin, Dash is the cryptocurrency that allows instantaneous and private transactions. Any user may contribute to the DAO network to get some Dash tokens in reward.

Symbol and Logo:

Currency code / Ticker symbol: DASH

Year of release: 2014

Website: https://www.dash.org/

Market capitalization (Feb 2018): $5.564 million

Mined Tokens (Feb 2018): 7.8 million DASH

> **Maximum Supply:** 18.9 million DASH
>
> **Source on Coinmarketcap:**
> https://coinmarketcap.com/currencies/dash/

A short story of Dash

Digital Cash - or simply, Dash - was worth 21 cents in early 2015, but today its value has stabilized above $1.000. If you had safely stored a few Dash tokens in a wallet back then, you would have thousands of dollars nowadays.

However, Dash's market price fluctuates rapidly - as any other cryptocurrency does. For instance, on December 20th, 2017 Dash's price peaked at around $1.600. Just two days later, on Dec 22nd, the market value dropped below $1.000 for a few hours.

Although this instability may discourage some newcomers, we cannot neglect the higher price that Dash is worth today. Let us review the reasons why this cryptocurrency has become so strong.

Digital Cash was initially a bitcoin fork, but nowadays the infrastructure has evolved far beyond its starting point; it has become a self-funded ecosystem for supporters and developers. In fact, anyone can contribute to the Dash network to earn tokens.

Dash has a self-funding ecosystem. Unlike bitcoin or most cryptocurrencies, the main strength of Dash is the community of users and developers who are funded by the system. The dev team holds +30 full-time employees.

Dash has lower fees than bitcoin. The two-layer Dash network allow the possibility of instantaneous transactions (InstantSend) and enables more privacy (PrivateSend) through the self-funded master nodes.

Dash is based on an active community. If autonomy in the infrastructure were not enough, there is also self-government through the internal voting system to solve disputes. Dash community can decide about anything, from reducing costs to hiring a new dev team.

Plus, to have a vote in the Dash network, you'd need to own a master node. Considering that each of these nodes is worth permanent 1.000 Dash tokens; there is no easy way to manipulate the networks will.

PrivateSend. Using a random bunch of the master nodes in the network, Dash user can efficiently mask their identity - if so they will. Given the permanent cost of 1.000 Dash tokens to own one master node, there is no cheap workaround to discover the identity of this cryptocurrency users. In February 2018, there are 4.785 active Dash master nodes.

InstantSend. Dash transactions occur in seconds. That is as instantaneous as it can go, right? You could buy literally buy drinks in a vending machine with Dash; there are no waiting times with this cryptocurrency thanks to the master nodes locks onto the input/outputs of tokens. What's more, this system prevents double spends with the tokens.

Governance functions. Dash's two-tier level structure makes it possible for people who provide value to the network to earn tokens as a salary. The mining level gets 45% block rewards, and so does the master node tier (servers with at least 1.000 tokens as regular funds).

Who could have forecast such a rapid growth when Dash was released at the price of 21 cents? A brilliant future awaits this cryptocurrency and the DAO backing it up. The market capitalization data places Dash in the 11th position in February 2018. This cryptocurrency has been hovering around the 10th position in the past few months.

#12 NEM

NEM works in a commercial blockchain platform, Mijin, which introduces the proof of importance (POI) technology, multisignature accounts, encrypted messaging and a reputation system.

> **Logo:**
>
> **Currency code / Ticker symbol:** XEM
>
> **Year of release:** 2015
>
> **Websites:** https://nem.io/
>
> **Market capitalization (Feb 2018):** $4.834 million
>
> **Circulating Tokens (Feb 2018):** 8.999 million XEM
>
> **Maximum Supply:** 8.999 million XEM
>
> **Source on Coinmarketcap:** https://coinmarketcap.com/currencies/nem/

A short story of NEM

The NEM project started on the Bitcoin Talk forum by a user called *UtopianFuture*. The original development was inspired by NXT. Initially, NEM was aimed to create a fork of NXT, but this was eventually dismissed.

An entirely new codebase was developed to create the new cryptocurrency. An open call for participation began on the Bitcoin Talk forum in early 2014. The main aim was to achieve a community-oriented cryptocurrency from the audience.

In April 2016, Tech Bureau, one of Japan's largest cryptocurrency exchanges, Zaif, created a partnership with NEM to develop an innovative blockchain platform. CoinCheck was the victim of a massive attack resulting in the loss of 523 million NEM tokens in January 2018. The tokens were worth around $534 million.

The security breach was caused by the lack of measures on CoinCheck's side. After that, the NEM dev team refused to conduct a hard fork. They are creating an automated tagging system to follow the money and label any account who could receive money from dubious sources.

#13 Monero

A cryptocurrency alternative solution to public vulnerability of the bitcoin ledger is Monero. Private, secure and untraceable transactions. Fungible digital tokens with decentralized distribution.

Logo:

Symbol: ɱ

Currency code / Ticker symbol: XMR

Year of release: 2014

Websites: https://getmonero.org/

Market capitalization (Feb 2018): $4.742 million

Mined Tokens (Feb 2018): 15.7 million XMR

Supply: 18.4 million XMR (then, 0.3 XMR per 1-minute block)

Source on Coinmarketcap: https://coinmarketcap.com/currencies/monero/

A short story of Monero

Monero has multiple operative system compatible clients which enable the privacy and decentralization of this altcoin. This digital asset has a public ledger, and the tokens must be mined with a more egalitarian process in comparison to the bitcoin mining algorithm.

Unfortunately, the privacy feature has drawn the attraction of malicious doers who seek a new means to avoid law enforcement. On the brighter side, the more equally-distributed mining process has allowed users to participate in the token creation.

This cryptocurrency has also attracted some malware developer's attention. The distributed mining effort is compatible with malware which enforces the victim's CPU to perform the tasks to create tokens in the background. Hence, the controversy around this digital token.

Moreover, the JavaScript implementation of Monero makes it possible to embed the mining algorithm in a website so that any visitor contributes to this process with computational resources. Neat, right? Of course, in this case, the user must accept the terms to contribute to this global effort to mine the Monero tokens remotely.

#14 Lisk

Forked from Crypti, regularly updated by an active JS dev team.

Logo:

Currency code / Ticker symbol: LSK

Year of release: 2016

Website: https://lisk.io/

Market capitalization (Feb 2018): $3.608 million

Mined Tokens (Feb 2018): 118.2 million LSK

Max Supply: 118.3 million LSK

Source on Coinmarketcap: https://coinmarketcap.com/currencies/lisk/

A short story of Lisk

Lisk is a public blockchain which was developed as a fork from Crypti in 2016. This cryptocurrency conducted its own ICO to raise funds which were distributed within the community. This ICO raised up to 14.000 BTC tokens – it was one of the most successful campaigns. Soon after, LSK was available for trading in the major exchanges.

There was a period when Lisk was a top cryptocurrency in the market. Each application has a side sidechain independent from the main Lisk blockchain. The central premise behind this feature is to allow more scalability in the dev projects. For instance, the sidechains make it possible to implement additional security measures that Lisk may not have without any incompatibility issues.

Lisk is programmed with NodeJS and JavaScript. Although JS is an interpreted language, the development is faster than programming in compiled languages. There are plenty of developers working in the programming languages that structure the Lisk core. Thus, there is a regular activity in the updates for this payment platform.

The Delegated Proof of Stake (DPoS) which runs in the LSK algorithm is an improvement of the POS available in other cryptocurrencies. Only the 101 top delegates in the network actively secure the system. The block processing time is just 10 seconds in Lisk. Any issue in a sidechain's app can be handled with a hard fork from that chain.

#15 TRON

The TRON Foundation developed the homonymous platform to reward programmers for sharing their blockchain applications.

Logo:

Currency code / Ticker symbol: TRX

Year of release: 2017

Website: https://tron.network/

Market capitalization (Feb 2018): $3.429 million

Mined Tokens (Feb 2018): 65.748 million TRX

Maximum Supply: 100.000 million TRX

Source on Coinmarketcap: https://coinmarketcap.com/currencies/tron/

A short story of TRON

The main idea which propelled the creation of TRON as an open source web 4.0 blockchain Dapp[4] platform was the content entertainment distribution. Any user in the platform may publish, store and own data. The long-term objective is to enable users to rely completely on this community for the services they use every day.

TRON is compatible with blockchain-based smart contracts. Users from all over the world have participated in the TRON environment, the web 4.0 ecosystem. What is the web 4.0 again? Let us review the succession of versions of the Internet quickly:

- **Web 1.0 Search Engines.** The first version of Yahoo.

- **Web 2.0 Social Media.** Facebook, Twitter, Wikipedia.

- **Web 3.0 The 3D experience.** The current version of the web with enhanced features, streaming and live connections.

- **Web 4.0 Ultra-intelligence.** Face recognition, intelligent apps, smart search, big data. All the good stuff together.

TRON is betting for the next step in the development of the online services. Developers and users collaborate with a digital economy.

---

[4] Decentralized application.

#16 Ethereum Classic

The fork of the Ethereum platform split the community into two groups. Ethereum Classic has the virtues of Ethereum with some additional features.

Logo:

Currency code / Ticker symbol: ETC

Year of release: 2016

Website: https://ethereumclassic.github.io/

Market capitalization (Feb 2018): $3.799 million

Mined Tokens (Feb 2018): 99.9 million ETC

Maximum Supply: 100 million ETC

Source on Coinmarketcap: https://coinmarketcap.com/currencies/ethereum-classic/

A short story of Ethereum Classic

In May 2016, a vulnerability was discovered in the Ethereum platform. Due to this weakness, 3.6 million ETH tokens were stolen. A venture capital fund called "The DAO" moved the tokens to another account without previous notification to the owners. Hence, there was a debate on how the situation should be handled in the community.

In July 2016, a vote took place to result in a hard fork of the Ethereum blockchain. The users who kept using the unforked version of Ethereum (the "older" tokens) are those who now have Ethereum Classic, hence the name. They were not in agreement with the hard fork as a solution to the issues in the community.

A few months later, the ETC blockchain had its own forks, in October 2016 and early 2017, respectively. By the end of 2017, the unlimited token emission was changed to a fixed cap of 210 million tokens. Ethereum Classic co-exists with the made-up unit called *gas*, which is used to quantify the number of resources that the processes need.

The applications that run without downtime, censorship, fraud or third-party participation are regulated by smart contracts in the platform. Recently, ETC has implemented a solution for the difficulty bomb and the replay attacks in the network.

#17 VeChain

VeChain innovation targets the Internet of Things (IoT) to revolutionize the supply chain assuring authenticity and quality.

Logo:

Currency code / Ticker symbol: VEN

Year of release: 2017

Websites: https://www.vechain.com/#/

Market capitalization (Feb 2018): $3.150 million

Mined Tokens (Feb 2018): 474.7 million

Maximum Supply: 873 million VEN

Source on Coinmarketcap: https://coinmarketcap.com/currencies/vechain/

A short story of VeChain

How could you know for sure the quality standards of a product you purchase? In the physical world, there are procedures to check the producers and distributors comply with such standards. For instance, the electronic devices are tested before a buyer makes use of it.

VeChain aims to introduce the same quality tests supported by the blockchain. The supply chain is one half of the entire queue; the products have radio-frequency identification (RFID) tags to check the authenticity. The validation is registered in the VeChain ledger.

Due to the spread of fake products distribution in many countries, there is a high interest in authentication processes. VeChain focuses on the verification of luxury items, wines, and automotive parts. However, the technology is not limited to these niches; it can be applied to any sector and almost any kind of product.

VeChain is currently hot due to the large number of partnerships that the platform has attracted in a rather short time. For instance, Direct Imported Goods (DIG), the most significant importer of high-class wine in China, has relied on VeChain to surpass the fake wine concern in the country. Also, Renault has implemented this blockchain in the distribution of their automotive parts to enforce genuineness. More partners have been announced to join the VeChain community soon.

#18 Qtum

The of blockchain as a service through Dapps and smart contracts is the central premise behind the development of the Qtum platform.

> **Logo:**
>
> **Currency code / Ticker symbol:** QTUM
>
> **Year of release:** 2017
>
> **Website:** https://qtum.org/en/
>
> **Market capitalization (Feb 2018):** $2.439 million
>
> **Mined Tokens (Feb 2018):** 73.8 million QTUM
>
> **Maximum Supply:** 100 million QTUM
>
> **Source on Coinmarketcap:** https://coinmarketcap.com/currencies/qtum/

A short story of Qtum

The QTUM Foundation developed the homonymous decentralized platform which is fully compatible with smart contracts and runs on multiple virtual machines. The network uses the POS algorithm to validate the operations. In a sense, QTUM combines the strengths of Bitcoin and Ethereum.

However, QTUM is more scalable than its counterparts. Having the best of both sides, QTUM can run any code or Dapp based on this blockchain without points of failure. The 100 million QTUM tokens were created and distributed in the crowd sale, among founders, backers and the dev team, and a stake (29%) was banked to fund community initiatives.

Although this cryptocurrency was released in 2017, the project already has a maximum presence. There are mobile wallets, browser and web wallets, desktop wallets, and even hardware wallets. Due to the 1% POS inflation, staking QTUM tokens rewards in the long-term.

The future of this blockchain platform and payment system looks promising. On one side, any development for the bitcoin can be implemented in QTUM, such as SegWit. Also, any Dapp or Ethereum-based smart contract is also fully compatible with this decentralized ecosystem. Having the best of both worlds has its advantages after all.

#19 Bitcoin Gold

Bitcoin Gold attempts to provide a user-friendly alternative to the corporative dominance that currently takes place in Bitcoin mining.

Logo:

Currency code / Ticker symbol: BTG

Year of release: 2017

Website: https://bitcoingold.org/

Market capitalization (Feb 2018): $2.357 million

Mined Tokens (Feb 2018): 16.8 million BTG

Maximum Supply: 16.9 million BTG

Source on Coinmarketcap: https://coinmarketcap.com/currencies/bitcoin-gold/

A short story of Bitcoin Gold

The forks of the Bitcoin have been developed to propose solutions to different issues in the original system. For instance, Bitcoin Cash handled the capacity limitations regarding the block size limit of 1MB (which was later increased slightly due to the implementation of SegWit). Bitcoin Gold is meant to offer a workaround to facilitate mining to any user regardless the computing power.

As the popularity of the bitcoin grew, the customized application-specific integrated circuits (ASIC) became more relevant to mine with more profit. Thus, the miners with more processing power have quicker access to the bitcoin tokens. BTG has an algorithm which does not profit from ASIC developments.

Bitcoin mining process is ruled by the SHA-256 algorithm, which is exigent in computing resources. On the other hand, Bitcoin Gold implements a POW algorithm known as Equihash, based on memory rather than computing stamina. The spirit of BTG is to present a profitable mining option to any user with limited resources.

Hence, the Bitcoin Gold initiative looks forward to being a more democratic system. However, controversy has surrounded the launch of BTG. Some people claim that Bitcoin Gold should not hold onto the bitcoin name, but others say that this is a legitimate cryptocurrency.

#20 Tether

Backed by one dollar for each token issued, Tether implements tokenized traditional currencies supported by governments.

Logo:

Symbol: ₮

Currency code / Ticker symbol: USDT

Year of release: 2015

Website: https://tether.to/

Market capitalization (Feb 2018): $2.214 million

Mined Tokens (Feb 2018): 2.217 million USDT

Maximum Supply: 2.280 million USDT

Source on Coinmarketcap: https://coinmarketcap.com/currencies/tether/

A short story of Tether

Tether introduced a platform to transact with traditional currencies in the way we are used to paying with digital assets. Isn't that great? That is just the beginning of the good news. Imagine being able to make transactions with fiat currency, such as USD, Euros, Yens, and others, with 1-to-1 tether support (1 USDT token for 1 monetary unit).

Although there is a fixed unit of account like traditional fiat currency, USDT has a different – and volatile – exchange rate with other cryptocurrencies. Although this digital asset has a fiat currency value, this is not a legal tender or a financial instrument. Thus, USDT has no contractual rights, legal claims or any guarantees against losses.

Moreover, the USDT is not available for trading in countries where digital assets are not regulated yet. But, there is also a bright side to the use of these tokens. USDT has an easy setup, API integration, complete support and wallet compatibility.

In fact, if you want a digital payment system, you can embrace USDT for the development of your app. The benefits of the blockchain applied to the fiat currencies is real thanks to Tether Limited. You can even make use of ATMs to get cash by transacting with this digital token. The future of this platform is looking exciting as of 2018.

Which cryptocurrency is worth mining in 2018?

This is probably the one-million-token question, right? When it comes to picking a digital asset for investment, there are a few factors to consider. You should think of cryptocurrency mining as a long-term investment.

Why do you need a long-term approach? Because in most cases you will not be banking a significant stake of tokens overnight. Mining takes time and demands computing resources. On top of that, you need to spend money on electricity – because there is no way to use a device without stepping on the bill.

The most crucial factors to consider or mining tokens are the following (ordered from the least to the most important):

- **Block time:** How much time does it take to process a block of data in the blockchain? The less time, the most blocks you will handle in a day. The more blocks, the more tokens you are likely to mine.

- **Block reward.** Think of this as a lottery. Each time a block is processed (e.g. added to the shared ledger), the contributors get tokens (or fractions of the unit) for their service. The higher the reward, the simpler it gets to get some (fractions of the) tokens.

- **Difficulty.** As the name claims, this is the complexity of the computing problems that your device will need to solve. The complexity is set so that all the miners have some equality in the token creation. However, in some ecosystems, the high difficulty benefits the most potent miners, such as the ASIC mining for Bitcoin. There are also some cryptocurrencies which have removed this barrier so that anyone can have chances to get the new tokens, like Bitcoin Gold.

- **Market value.** The current price of the cryptocurrency is always a volatile reference. There is no way to tell how much a given token will be worth tomorrow. So, *how can you be influenced by a constantly-changing price?*

- Although there is a random character to the evolution of the market price, the supporters of a given asset provide the background that is crucial to make the project grow. Hence, you should study the backers instead of the price: *Are they promising in the long run?* In case they are, the price will eventually ramp up.

- Plus, their founders of the token development are also relevant in this aspect. If they have a clear roadmap and work with the organization, chances are they will make the ecosystem improve. There are too many cryptocurrency projects running today, not all of them are likely to succeed. You should always study the background of a token before investing your own money.

- **Profitability.** Is the token value high enough to give you benefit in the mining? If you are willing to mine Bitcoin, you'd better have an ASIC device. You cannot get any profit with a regular computer with this cryptocurrency. However, you could try others.

  There is an updated source of profitability information at http://whattomine.com/.

- **Electricity.** Last but definitely not least, there is the electricity bill. Depending on where you are based, you could have adverse profitability just because of this factor. Even with an ASIC, you may not be mining bitcoin tokens if the price per kWh is too high in your city.

What is the price of electricity worldwide?

There are countries with low-priced electricity and some with a much higher kWh price. In 2011, the cheapest country (electricity-wise) was India, with USD8¢ per kWh. The most expensive county was Denmark, with no less than USD41¢ per kWh. Quite a difference, right?

As of 2018, the prices in Europe ranged from USD12¢ in Bulgaria to USD38¢ in – you guessed it – Denmark. So, at least we know for sure where it cannot be profitable to mine tokens. On the bright side, the kWh price has stabilized around the USD20¢ zone in the UK. But, things get better overseas, where the kWh electricity prices ramped up from USD6.6¢ to USD10.3¢ in the USA (from 1990 to 2016).

Having the worldwide rates in mind, it's not looking too bad. In 2018, you can still find lower prices in the USA, but it depends drastically on where you are based. You'd better not move to Alaska to mine bitcoins at a USD21.5¢ per kWh bill – at least you would not have cooling issues there!

Louisiana (USD9.3¢ / kWh) and Washington (USD9.6¢ / kWh) had the lowest prices in 2017. What determines the cost of the electricity? The following factors are the most influential:

- **Time of usage.** There are companies which offer a discount for consumption during off-peak hours.

- **Month.** Summer is more expensive than winter overall.

- **Location.** As we have seen, the place where you are living is a deciding factor in the electricity prices.

- **Consumption.** Different rates apply depending on the power you will need.

- **Provider.** Each company has one's own prices.

Therefore, unless you have the chance to get *cheap* electricity, you will not have profitability in the mining. Consider that the devices should be working for several hours on a regular basis to mine tokens. An option is to get a commercial rate for the electricity, but in that case, you should have a business approach to the mining of tokens.

In my opinion, before deciding which cryptocurrency to mine, you should have a plan to access cheap-by-your-country-standards electricity. Then, you should study which asset is worth your investment.

What to mine?

That is indeed the question. Of course, everyone is willing to mine bitcoin tokens or possibly one of the other top 5 cryptocurrencies (Ethereum, Ripple, Bitcoin Cash, or Litecoin). Those are the most supported tokens which plenty of room for trading. Let us focus on those assets first.

What do you need to mine Bitcoin?

We already know how valuable bitcoin tokens are. Even after the descent of the price in Dec17 / Jan18, each token is already worth over USD12.000 again as of February 2018. Hence, getting some BTC tokens is still a right approach in the long run. You will eventually have the chance to trade profitably.

However, mining bitcoin tokens are profitable if and only if you invest enough money in getting it done. You can get an estimation of your profit with this bitcoin mining calculator. There, you can input your electricity kWh rate (check a recent bill to have this parameter handy) so that you get a realistic estimation.

Another crucial parameter is the hash rate (the number of mining operations your device can process per second), though. The default value of that calculator is 14.000 Gh/s, which corresponds to an ASIC mining device, the AntMiner S9 which costs USD2.400.

At a price of USD10¢ per kWh, you'd be making USD5.044 yearly at the cost of USD1.200, so your profit would be around USD3.843. Not too bad for just having the device turned on working on its own, right? Well, the calculation considers the current mining difficulty for the estimation. Needless to say, that there is no way to know for sure if the complexity will get higher in the future – there is always the chance.

Hash rate

14000.0   Gh/s

In other words, unless you have a compelling device, you will have the slightest chance of making profitable mining for Bitcoin. And even so, all the possibilities aren't with you. Currently, the AntMiner S9 is the most powerful device to mine bitcoin tokens. If another device showed up in the market, e.g. the AntMiner S11, the current device would become less profitable; it would eventually render not profitable unless free electricity is accessible.

Fortunately, there is no S11 in the foreseeable future, not yet. So, the changing difficulty is the most concerning profitability-changing factor in the long run. The expected yearly profitability would reach $3.233 at USD15¢ per kWh, and just USD2.640 if you paid USD20¢

per kWh – arguably the worst-case scenario in the USA.

Wonder what would happen in Denmark? At USD40¢ per kWh, you'd get $231 in a year. I don't see anyone making a living mining Bitcoin with that forecast.

Will Bitcoin mining become "more difficult"?

Coming back to the difficulty, the trend is *growing* steadily. Although this parameter also fluctuates, given the current interest in the mining, there is no optimistic way of seeing the complexity descending to the ground. Moreover, the difficulty is tuned so that the block generation stays at 600 seconds to assure the same data flow in the network.

See why it grows? Since more mining devices join every day, the only way to keep the block generation time constant is by making it *more difficult* for the miners to process the hashes. One factor is closely related to the other. If tomorrow most people stopped mining, we could eventually use our phones to mine the tokens.

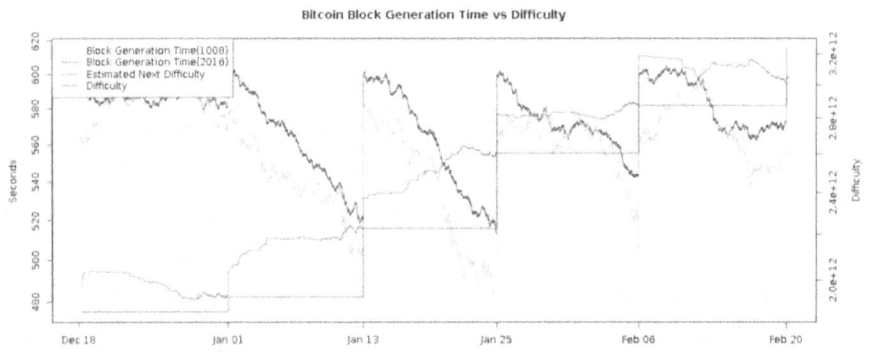

Source: https://bitcoinwisdom.com/bitcoin/difficulty

However, the real difficulty changes periodically after every 2016 blocks generated. Therefore, we can see that some of these updates have a descend in difficulty. Don't get excited, though, since most of them have a growing tendency.

Dec 18 2017	1,873,105,475,221	17.74%	13,408,211,263 GH/s
Dec 06 2017	1,590,896,927,258	18.11%	11,388,083,790 GH/s
Nov 24 2017	1,347,001,430,558	-1.28%	9,642,211,820 GH/s
Nov 10 2017	1,364,422,081,125	-6.09%	9,766,913,694 GH/s
Oct 26 2017	1,452,839,779,145	21.39%	10,399,832,230 GH/s
Oct 15 2017	1,196,792,694,098	6.49%	8,566,975,802 GH/s

Source: https://bitcoinwisdom.com/bitcoin/difficulty

Most updates have a green % increase, and you can see how the hash rate has also been increasing lately with a few exceptions. More people join the complex task of mining bitcoin tokens regularly.

Feb 20 2018	3,007,383,866,429	4.62%	21,527,692,255 GH/s
Feb 06 2018	2,874,674,234,415	10.43%	20,577,719,706 GH/s
Jan 25 2018	2,603,077,300,218	16.84%	18,633,553,122 GH/s
Jan 13 2018	2,227,847,638,503	15.36%	15,947,554,580 GH/s
Jan 01 2018	1,931,136,454,487	3.10%	13,823,613,194 GH/s
Dec 18 2017	1,873,105,475,221	17.74%	13,408,211,263 GH/s

Source: https://bitcoinwisdom.com/bitcoin/difficulty

Check the exponential growth of the parameters in a 9-month graphic.

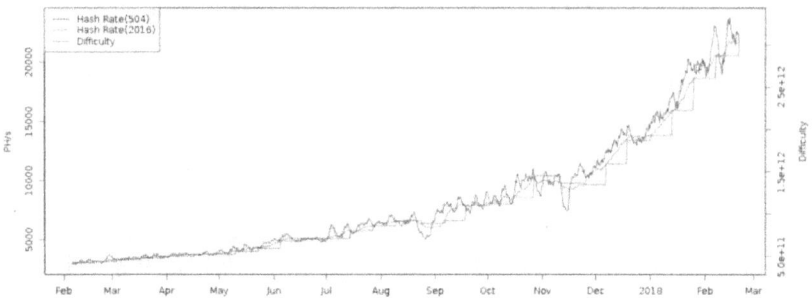

Source: https://bitcoinwisdom.com/bitcoin/difficulty

To sum up, you need a USD2.400 minimal investment to get started in this venture with chances to get your money back in less than a year. In fact, if you paid for more than one AntMiner S9, you'd still get the investment done since each miner is independent. You would get double the tokens with two miners, triple BTC tokens for three of them, and so on. Sadly, the expenses will increase in proportion, too.

The above images show the global effort to invest in bitcoin mining. There are industrial mining facilities which include several S9 devices with cooling systems. In most cases, this is an additional investment to make unless you have cooling options at your place.

Mining Bitcoin is profitable but expensive. I don't see the worldwide cryptocurrency community abandoning the bitcoin anytime soon, and you?

What do you need to mine Ethereum?

Ethereum is meant to be mined with graphics processor units (GPU). When picking the best one to mine this cryptocurrency, you should look at three deciding factors: price, hash rate, and power consumption. One of the top GPUs for this purpose is the AMD Radeon RX Vega 64, which can be adapted to mine at 41 MH/s consuming 135 Watts.

To have the right perspective about these features, check the specifications of the following top GPUs to mine ETH:

- Radeon RX Vega 56 computes 31 MH/s consuming 190 W.

- GeForce GTX 1080 TI processes 32 MH/s using 200W.

- Radeon RX 580 reaches 25 MH/s consuming 175 W.

- Radeon RX 480 can handle 24 MH/s requiring 170 W.

- GeForce GTX 1070 computes 27 MH/s using 200 W.

However, those are stock features. There are unique settings for each of the above GPUs which allow more processing power with less power consumption. These modifications are spread within the miner's community who are always tweaking the processors to get more juice out of them.

Having one GPU is the way to get started, but the most advanced miners have quite a few of these processors. How do they manage to mine with more than one GPU? They often build what is called a mining rig. The setup has a similar appearance to this:

Source: https://cryptosrus.com/ethereum-mining-rig/

As you can see, you need some parts to create this baby, namely: a case, a power supply, a motherboard, some wires, and, of course, the GPUs. When you have these many processors working for prolonged times, it is also recommended to have a box fan next to them working to provide the air circulation for cooling.

Such a setup is a long-term inversion, but it can prove to be not too profitable in the long run. Of course, the main advantage of having a pro setup like a mining rig is that you can turn to mining other cryptocurrencies in the future with the same GPUs. As time goes one, Ethereum mining may be less profitable, so having a versatile setup is the best strategy.

In fact, some experts recommend opting for less popular cryptocurrencies for GPU mining due to the saturation in ETH network. In the past months, is has been commented that Ethereum will change the algorithm based on POW to POS. The reason being the colossal saturation of the network of this cryptocoin.

Among the highly profitable GPU-minable cryptocurrencies, you have Pirl, Nicehash, and Ethereum Classic.

What do you need to mine Ripple?

Not all the cryptocurrencies work the same way. Since Bitcoin and Ethereum have different mining specifications, it is natural to ask about the third cryptocurrency in the market capitalization market, Ripple. But this coin cannot be mined. The XRP tokens already exist, but they are not circulating in the public market at this moment.

Ripple Labs, the responsible company for this cryptocurrency, decided that the sudden flood of tokens would harm the current inversions in this ecosystem. So, they opted to have a significant amount of the tokens in an escrowed account which releases a certain number periodically. Neat, huh?

Each escrow will expire every first day of the month during the next four years releasing 1 billion XRP tokens monthly. Ripple Labs will be able to distribute the tokens as rewards to the community or send them to institutional investors. In the case that the tokens were not used, they would be placed in an escrow extending the most distant expiration date of the contract.

The success of the Ripple depends on the institutional interest that this cryptocurrency may attract. You can already make use of XRP tokens to make quick transfers that are much agiler than those with other cryptocurrencies. Whenever you need speed and low fees, Ripple is the way to go.

However, this cryptocurrency is not meant to be the universal payment system. Instead, it offers a means to make fiat transactions more versatile. Banks have shown interest in the use of XRP for the operations. In the case that this trend continued, we will see many more of the XRP tokens circulating in the public network.

A mining-free ecosystem has its own advantages in comparison with the saturation of the top two cryptocurrencies, Bitcoin and Ethereum. In any case, being number three in market capitalization is not that bad, is it?

What do you need to mine Bitcoin Cash?

Bitcoin Cash is very similar to Bitcoin in the main specifications. The price of this token has been on the rise for a long time. Moreover, the difficulty in the mining is not as high as for bitcoin tokens. You need rough computational power to be on the profitable side of the mining with BCH, just like happens with the Bitcoin.

If you have a somehow outdated Bitcoin-mining ASIC, it could be more profitable with computing BCH tokens nowadays. After all, fewer miners are working on the latter than they are on trying to get BTC tokens. One thing is clear; you cannot get profit with regular devices.

If you can afford to create a rig for BCH mining, you could start to bank some tokens. However, the inversion is high due to the similarities with the original cryptocurrency. Mining this token may not be an easy task in the future.

What do you need to mine Litecoin?

Just as the other top cryptocoins, Litecoin may be a challenge for newcomers to the mining activities. First, you will need an ASIC to get profit out of this activity. Hence, you will need to invest in the hardware to get started in the mining with LTC.

This token demands the Scrypt algorithm for computational mining tasks. One deciding factor for this process is the RAM and graphics card RAM in the device which will mine the tokens. You will also need a cooling system to keep the processors at an acceptable temperature.

Then, you can use this profitability calculator to determine if the mining will be worth it for your case. You need to input the specs of your hardware and the electricity cost in your city to have this calculation performed.

WhatToMine.com

This website is one of the most visited sources of information when checking the latest updates about the mining profitability. You can see the status of the cryptocurrencies within seconds. Also, you can make forecasts of the profitability which may come along with mining tasks for a given cryptocoin.

Whenever you want to have a look at the mining situation, you can look at this site. In a glance, you will know the expected profitability of the mining for each cryptocurrency according to your electricity expenses and hash rate.

Short roadmap for new bitcoin users

Making investments with cryptocurrencies is always like using a double-edged sword. You never know if you will be earning money tomorrow or losing it instead.

However, I think that contrary to the regular stock market, you should not only use a win/lose criterion. In the short run, you could potentially "lose" a fraction of your investment due to fluctuations, but this tendency will eventually be over.

Thus, you can choose the perfect time to sell those tokens for a better price. Of course, you should not invest all your savings to the latest cryptocurrency in the market which looks more relaxed than the others. Making risky moves is not the way to go with cryptocoins, either.

There is also no room for the safest strategies. According to my experience, you can track the bitcoin price 24/7 and still risk losing some revenue due to market fluctuations. Why? Because you may not be able to wait for the best moment to sell or buy.

Nobody knows when that perfect moment is. Besides, if you need to get some of your money back with urgency, you do not have room for patients. Thus, investing in cryptocurrencies should not take the significant part of your savings.

Instead, you should make use of an amount of money you could "lose". That's why I always recommend starting slow, getting the basics of the market before making a more in-depth immersion. It's still better to be safe than sorry when it comes to your money.

There are plenty of websites, authors and "gurus" who claim that you will always have profit with the bitcoin. That is not the case. What you can do is assure you take part in this revolution, but if you are willing to make a safe move only, then the cryptocurrency sector is not the place for you.

Risk will always be involved in this market because the prices change according to complex and random human decisions worldwide. Nobody can foresee how those decisions will alter the bitcoin market the next day.

However, it's an exciting sector to be involved in nonetheless. By following tips of experienced users, you will be in the safe zone. Besides, always make sure to learn the procedures by yourself with small amounts of money involved.

Why risk sending 0.1 BTC tokens to a wrong wallet if you can master the process with 0.00000001 BTC instead? That's what I mean by learning in small quantities first. Then, you will master the basics when the times comes to send and receive more significant amounts of tokens.

There is no hurry, no shortcuts and no magic recipe for success. As in any other aspect of the real world, you will get profit only by working hard and being constant in the learning. Try to keep up-to-date with the latest trends in the sector to avoid issues with your tokens.

Also, make use of proved and well-supported tools only. Do not risk losing your tokens just to try a system which is not updated. Never risk your inversion for a gamble.

In the end, you will know enough to make your own educated decisions. May the cryptocoins be with you.

Conclusion

Thank you again for downloading this book!

The scope of this book is ambitious although there is a lot to be said about the topic. Nowadays, we are witnessing the relentless growth of the crypto market and its diffusion in more niches.

The bitcoin is the leading asset of this new digital revolution with unforeseeable repercussions for the global economy. It is yet soon to know how far the cryptos will move on.

Some experts claim that the bitcoin will eventually fade into oblivion. Others say that this is a temporary fashion. On the other hand, the enthusiasts state that the cryptos will compete toe-to-toe with the traditional currencies.

No matter the long-term outcome, we are currently living in a continually changing period. Thus, understanding the blockchain, the bitcoin, and the related tools is an essential skill to make right calls whenever you are involved with them.

Because you will eventually run into the opportunity of trading cryptos even if you do not actively look for the chance. Everyone is invited to take part in this revolution of the digital era.

I hope this book was able to help you to understand how the bitcoin revolution has changed the way we think of currencies. This digital development has come to stay for a long time.

The next step is to keep learning about trading and mining. It is your call to decide how to participate in the crypto sector. Whether you are just a casual user or an active contributor, now you can make an educated choice.

Thank you and good luck with your cryptos purchases!

Appendices

The following tutorials are meant to get you started in the – safe – use of the Bitcoin or any other cryptocurrency. The Electrum desktop wallet is one of the most recommended clients for PC – it is entirely safe and gets regular updates from the dev team. Moreover, using this client comes along with complete support from the community.

Groestlcoin is an example of an altcoin which can be mined from any device. Therefore, you can quickly get a stake of these tokens without a high-end computer. Plus, you can also install this wallet client on mobile and other operative systems aside from Windows, such as Linux or Mac. This multiplatform compatibility allows you to have access to your tokens from any device.

How to create a new Groestlcoin (GRS) standard wallet with the Electrum-GRS 2.5.4 in Windows 10

1. Double click on Select the installation path for the Electrum-GRS, wallet client. The default path will do in most cases, just click on Install to continue. To pick a different path, click on Browse to search for the location.

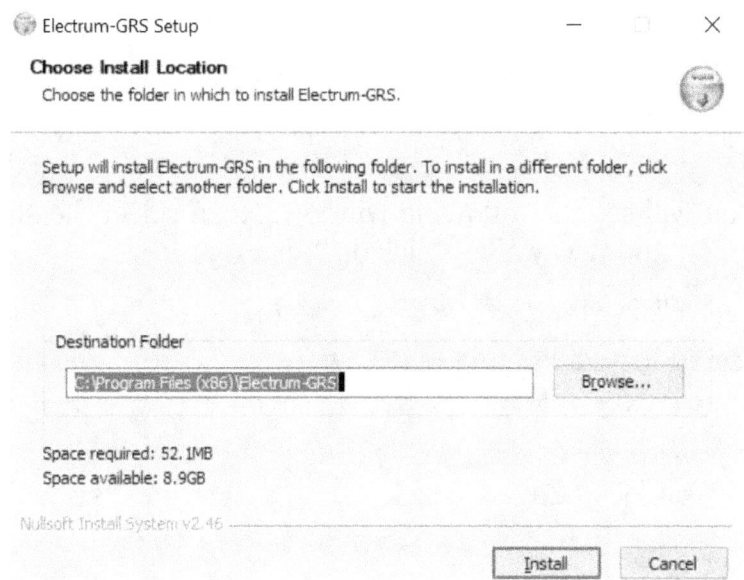

2. When the installation finishes, click on Close to proceed. The wallet client will be ready for the first set up. This process will take some minutes only, and you will need a piece of paper and a pen to secure your passphrase.

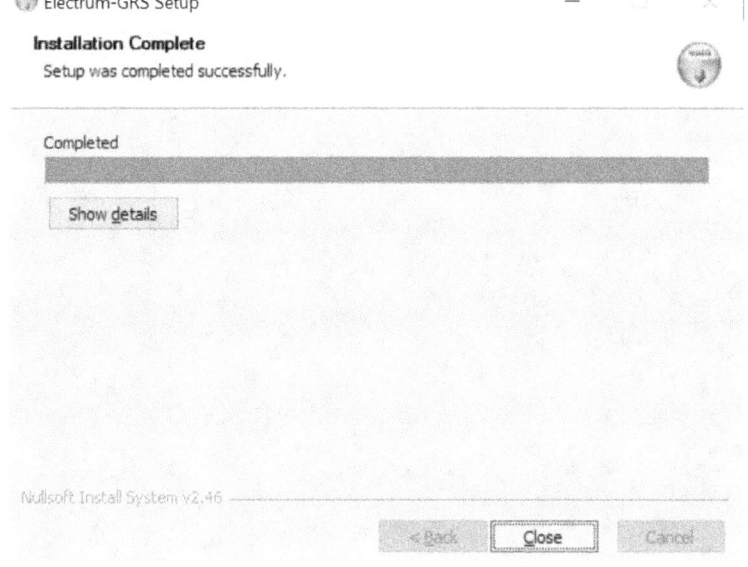

Patrick Wilder

3. Now, open the Electrum-GRS client to proceed. You can search the clients from the Home button or by double-clicking on the quick launcher.

4. You will see the following window. Next, select the standard wallet and new wallet. Click on Next to proceed.

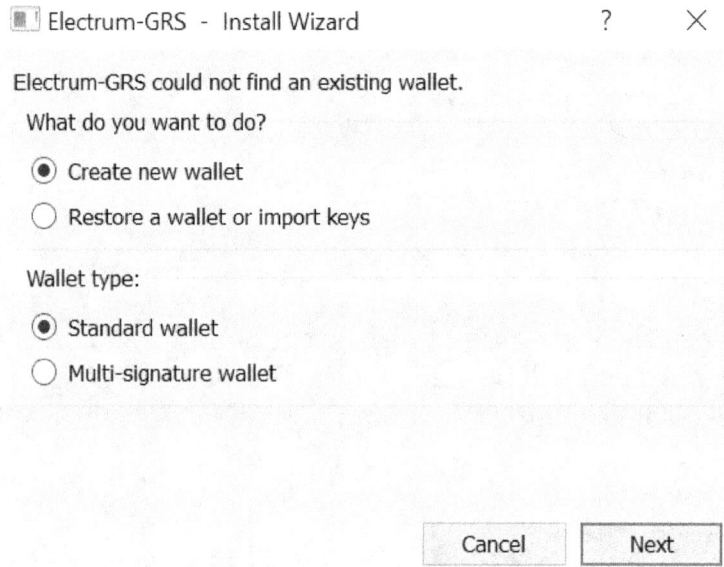

5. You will look at your recovery phrase now. Make sure to note it down in the paper. Store this phrase in a safe place.

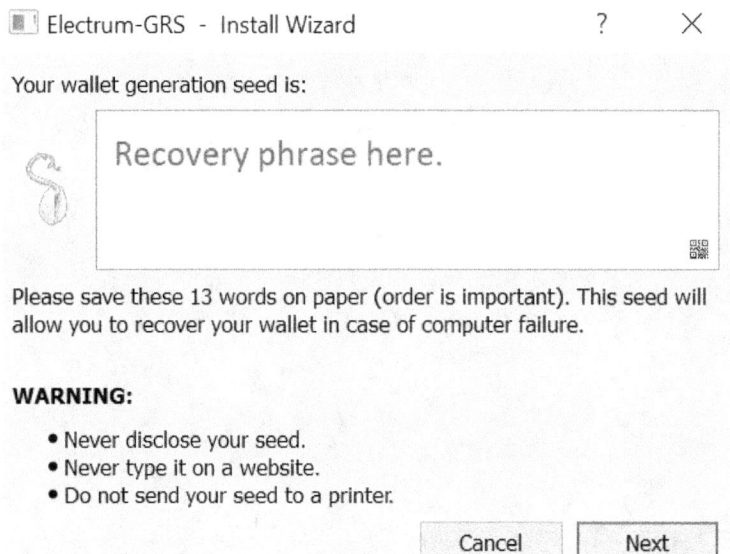

6. Then, you will have to input your recovery phrase to validate the previous step. Simply, type the recovery phrase (careful to the order of the words) and click on Next.

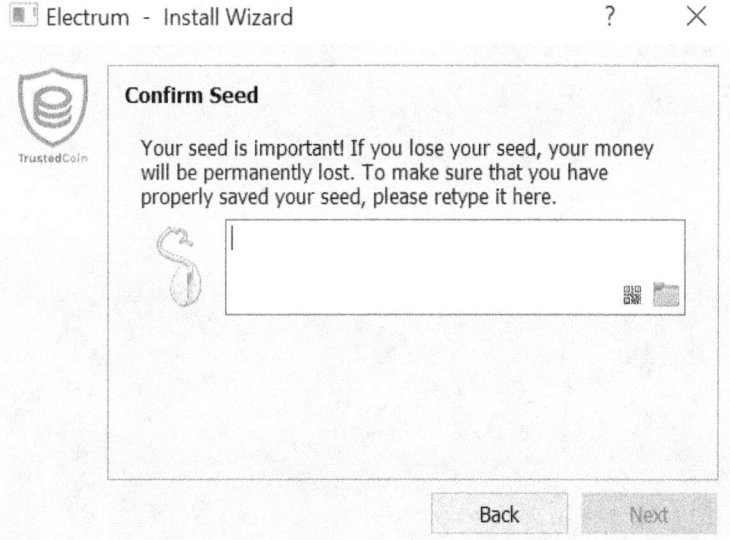

7. Create a secure password and confirm it. Also, note the password down. You can get a reliable password here.

8. Select the auto-connect feature and click Next to continue.

9. And you are all set to send and receive GRS safely!

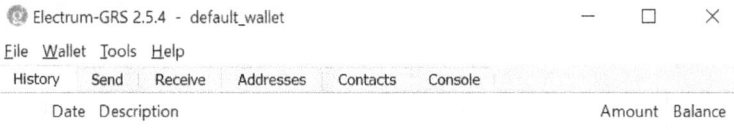

10. Go to Tools > Preferences to verify the following settings to have the wallet set up.

11. Restart the Electrum-GRS wallet client to see the settings. Advice: in the case that the wallet was not connected to the server, it may be due to a port issue. This is the online appearance of the client:

If the circle is red, you are offline. Then, go to Tools > Network, untick Use SSL and click on OK to apply the settings. Now, the wallet should be online.

How to create a new two-step authentication Bitcoin (BTC) wallet with the Electrum 3.0.6 client in Windows 10

This is a step-by-step guide to install the Electrum client (BTC wallet) on your PC. Like in the previous guide to create a standard wallet, you should try this setting on your personal computer only. This tutorial extends some of the steps of the previous one – in particular, we review the two-step authentication to prevent anyone from having access to your precious tokens (they should need to have access to your Google account, too!).

Although it's entirely optional, the two-step authentication is recommended. You will be surprised at how simple it is to increase the security of your wallets with a simple gesture. In other words, the two-step authentication is worth to try whenever possible. Note that not every developing team has enabled this enhanced feature in their wallet clients. There are also mobile clients with fingerprint scans to improve the security of the user.

1. Download the executable file here. As you can see, there is compatibility with the most popular operative systems, select the standard executable or the Windows installer to proceed:

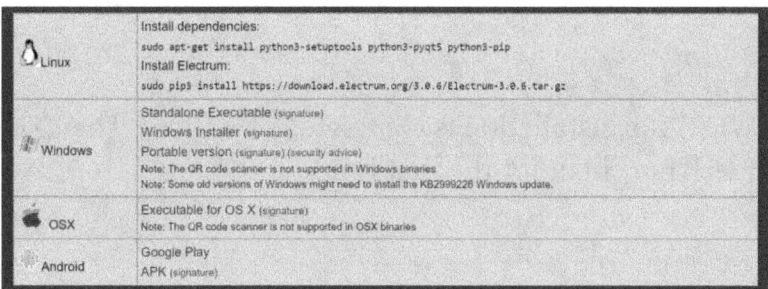

We will continue the installation of Windows 10. Find the downloaded .exe and double-click on it.

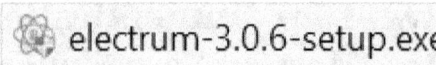

2. You will see a prompt to confirm the execution of the third-party executable. Click on Yes to continue. Don't worry, as long as you have downloaded the installers from the official site; your PC is safe.

3. Now, click on Install to start the process. And, grab a seat, this will take a while to complete.

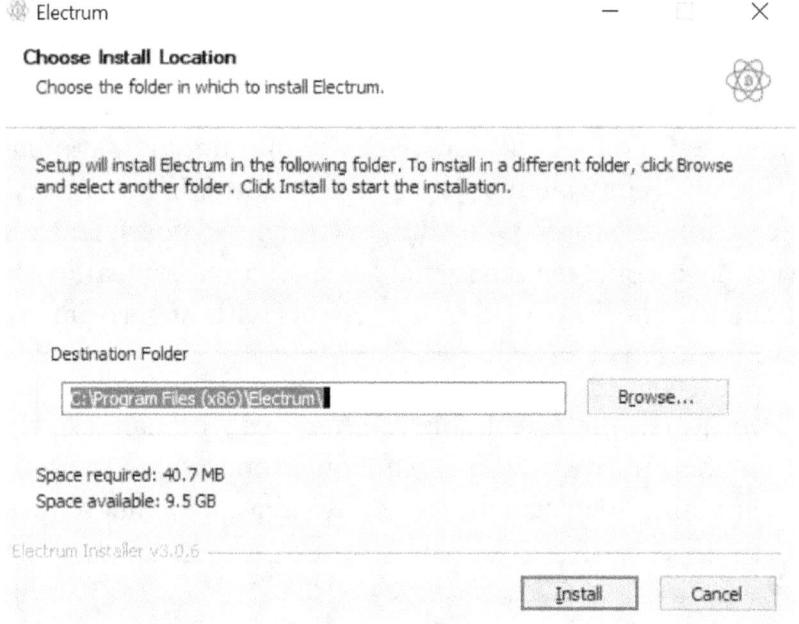

4. When the installation is complete, click Close. Then, open the Electrum client for the first time.

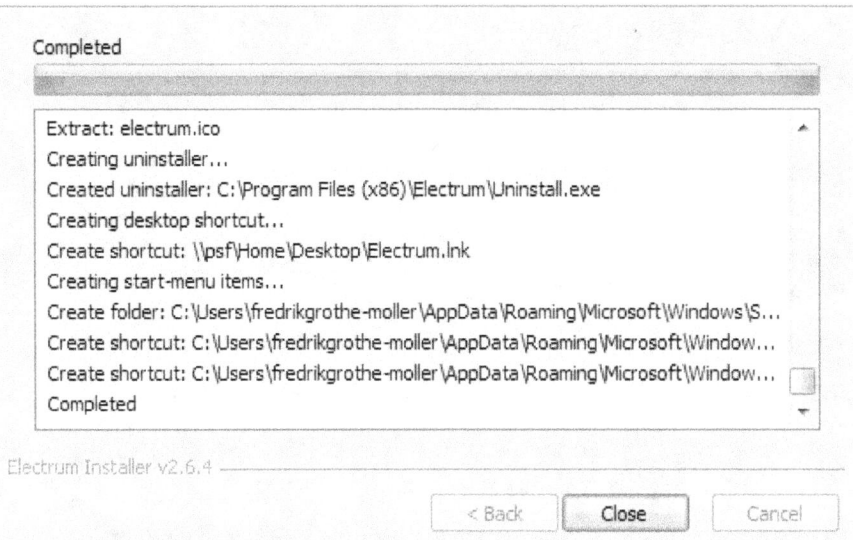

5. Click on the desktop icon or the menu icon to open the application.

Desktop quick launcher:

Menu icon:

6. Then, the Electrum client will open. You will be asked for the wallet's name. If you do not have a choice, then just click on Next. This decision will not compromise your security.

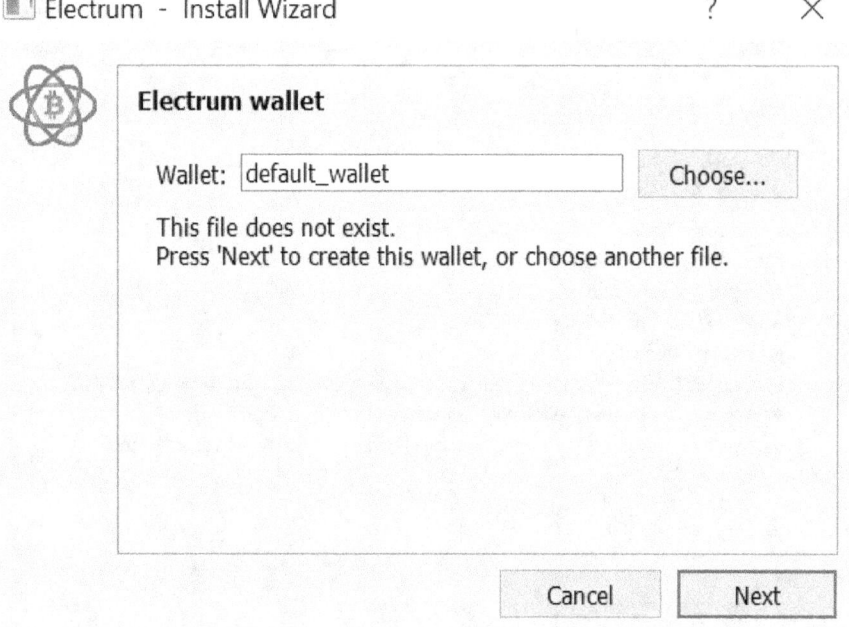

7. You can create a new wallet or restore a previous one on this step. Since this is your first wallet, just click Next to proceed.

8. Now, you can pick the type of wallet you prefer:

- **Standard:** the primary wallet without enhanced security.
- **Two-factor authentication:** the wallet we will create below, connected to the Google Authenticator app.
- **Multi-signature wallet:** for several users.
- **Import Bitcoin address:** to install a wallet of your own (if you already had one) in this client.

9. If you want more security, you should pick the two-factor authentication wallet. You will see a disclaimer now, click next to accept the terms. This is just a formality about the terms of use. You can, of course, read the terms carefully. **TL; DR:** they will not be responsible if you lose your BTC tokens for a human mistake or viruses on your device. If you mess up, it's your own responsibility. That said, being careful is harder than expected to make mistakes when using BTC tokens for transactions.

10. In this step, you should decide whether to create a new seed or restore a previous one. Click on create a new seed to get a brand-new wallet in this client. The seed is the recovery phrase you will get in the next step, which is a precious piece of information you should always protect. Never allow anyone to see this passphrase since anybody can install your wallet in another device with only this seed – unless the two-step authentication is enabled.

Cryptocurrency Masterclass 2018

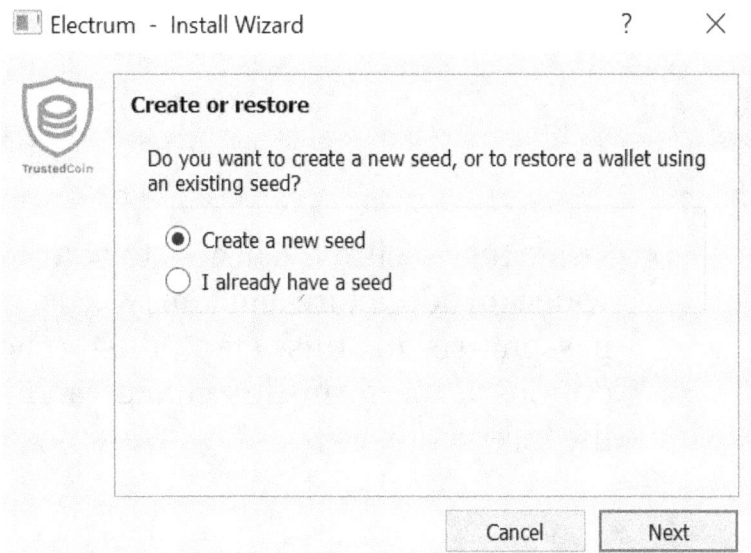

11. Now, get a pencil and a piece of paper **(preferably, use a notebook to avoid losing this information)** to note down the passphrase you will see. This is not a drill; you should be old-fashioned in this step.

12. Warning: you should keep this recovery passphrase safe to prevent that anyone else restores your wallet – ever. It is recommended not to store this information in a digital environment to make it impossible for anyone to have remote access.

👍 To further secure the access to your tokens, you can add more custom words to this passphrase in this step. Just, click on options to perform this change and follow the instructions.

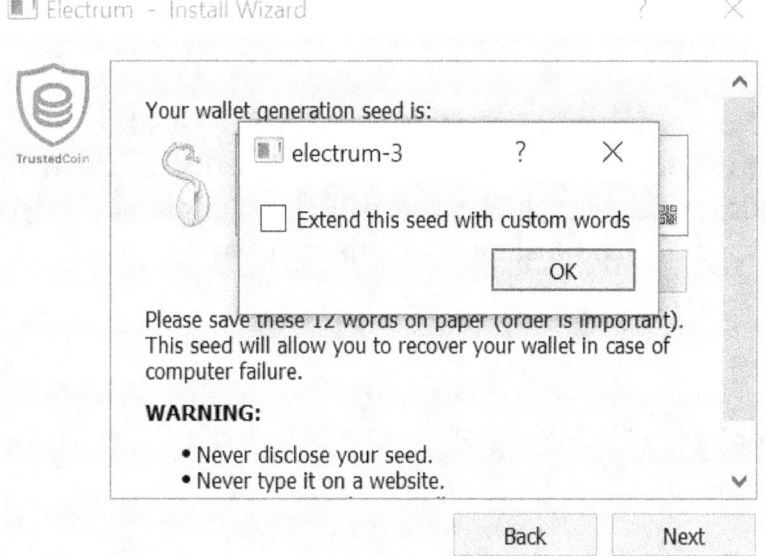

👍 **Remember that order is essential.**

Please save these 12 words on paper (order is important). This seed will allow you to recover your wallet in case of computer failure.

👍 **Once again, keep in mind:**

WARNING:

- Never disclose your seed.
- Never type it on a website.
- Do not store it electronically.

👍 **Really.** Follow the above pieces of advice to the letter.

13. Next, you will confirm your see (recovery phrase). Simply, type the seed (careful to the word order) to validate your backup notes.

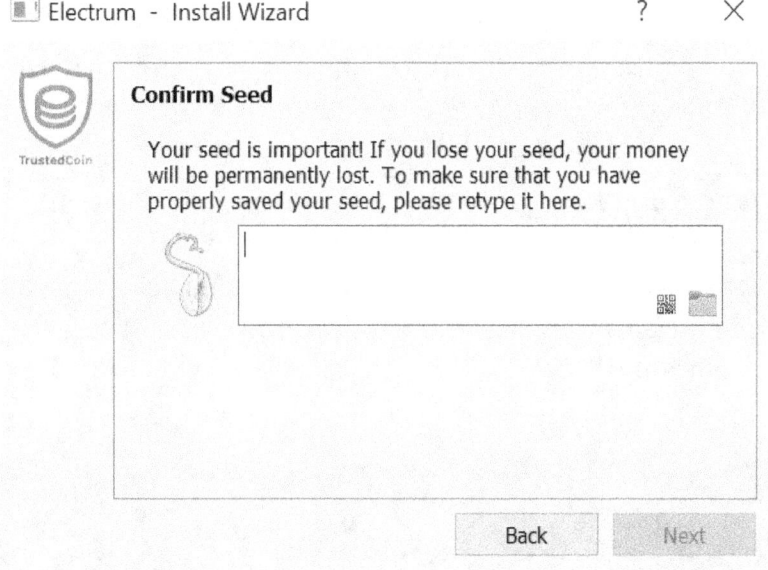

14. If the previous confirmation is complete, you will see this window. Now, you should create a password.

👍 This is a <u>password generator</u> which can provide crazy-strong strings according to the settings (mark all of them for more ~~fun~~

security). Check the password length settings; you could have an unbelievable long string:

Unbelievable

256
512
1024
2048

👍 Pick the length of the password. Keep in mind that the more extended, the harder to type. Starting at 16 characters, you are in the safer zone.

Password Length: | 16

15. It is also important to note that you should keep this password safe at all moments, too. Note it down and save it <u>on paper</u> preferably.

16. Click on Next to see the route where your wallet will be stored in your device. It is essential to know the location of your wallet in case you will need to move it to another device in the future. As you can see in the instructions, it is **necessary to have an internet connection** to proceed.

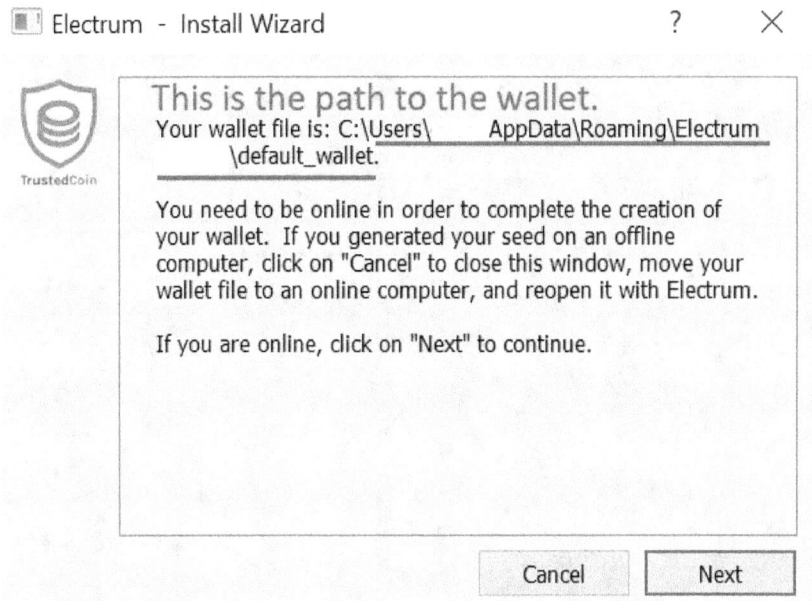

Your Windows username will appear in the blank spaces.

17. Now, you may input your e-mail address to link this wallet. You can also send and receive BTC tokens with an e-mail address in some exchanges and clients.

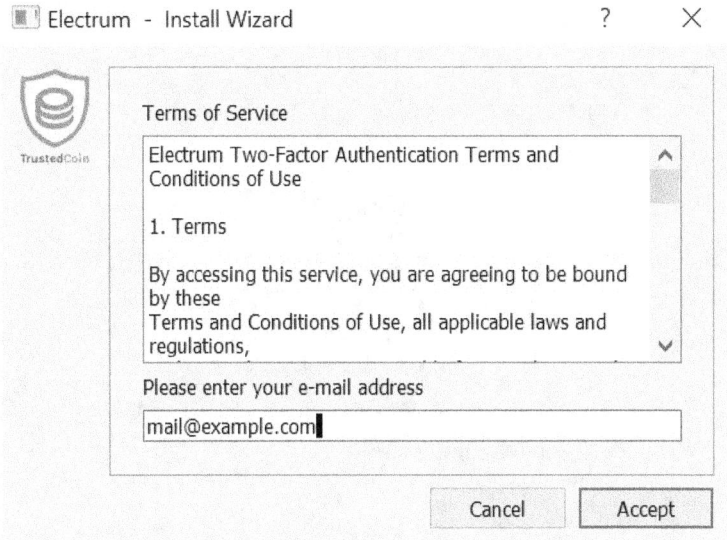

18. [You will not see the window below if you picked a standard wallet] **In the case that you had a Gmail account, you will be asked to use Google Authenticator to add an extra layer of protection. Just, follow the instructions to link the application with your wallet. You can download Google Authenticator** here. **You can also make use of Google Authenticator on PC, but you will need a Google account to get started. You have more information on** this post.

19. Once you have set up Google Authenticator, you will be asked to scan the QR code or input the key (above the QR code). Just, follow the steps to validate this step. And you are done! Now, you will see the following window, the Electrum client.

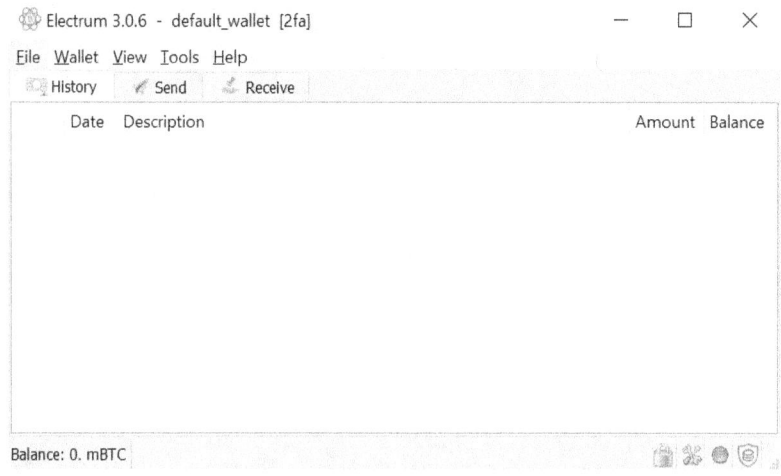

20. From this moment, you will be able to send and receive BTC

tokens using the Electrum client.

- **Send BTC.** This option is quite straightforward; you may input the BTC address, include a description of the transaction and select the amount. Note that the fee will determine how quick the transaction is processed, the lower the fee, the more time it will take to get confirmations.

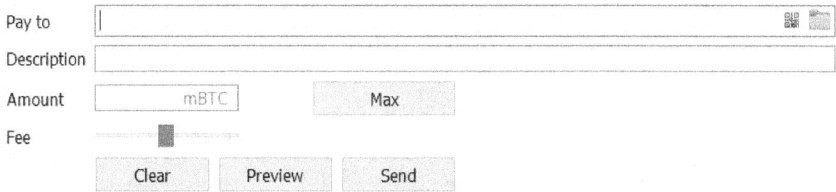

- **Receive BTC.** You can create a request to receive a payment with these options: a description, the requested amount (mBTC), and the expiration time.

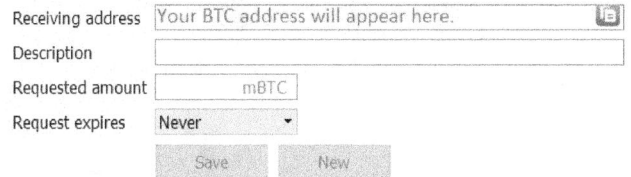 

Last steps: basic wallet configuration

1. Click on Tools > Preferences.

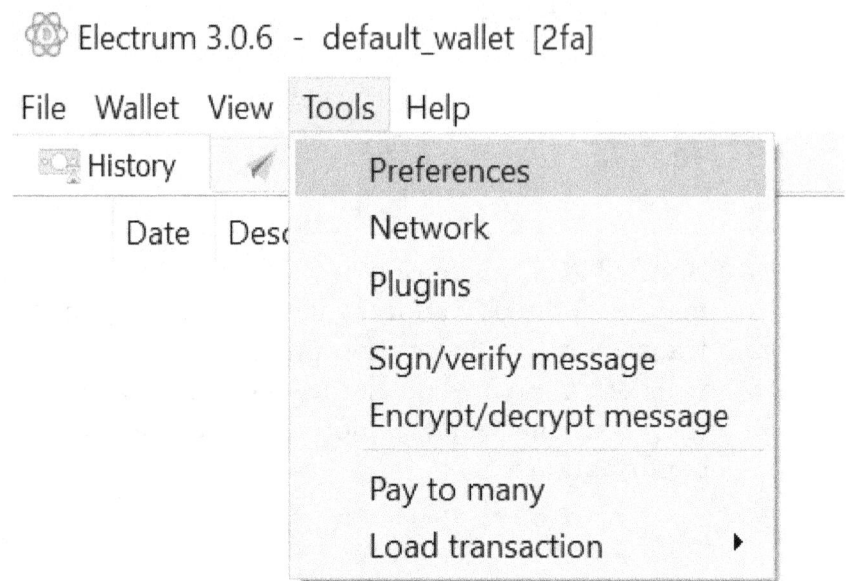

2. Then, click on Appearance Tab. Select your language (English by default), and pick 8 digits after the decimal point. You can also choose the base unit – my preference is BTC, but you can also use mBTC or bits. Moreover, you can use a block explorer for the transactions (e.g. a website where you will be directed to see how the confirmations evolve). You can try the explorer by yourself. I recommend Tradeblock.com. Click on Close to look at the changes applied to the Electrum client.

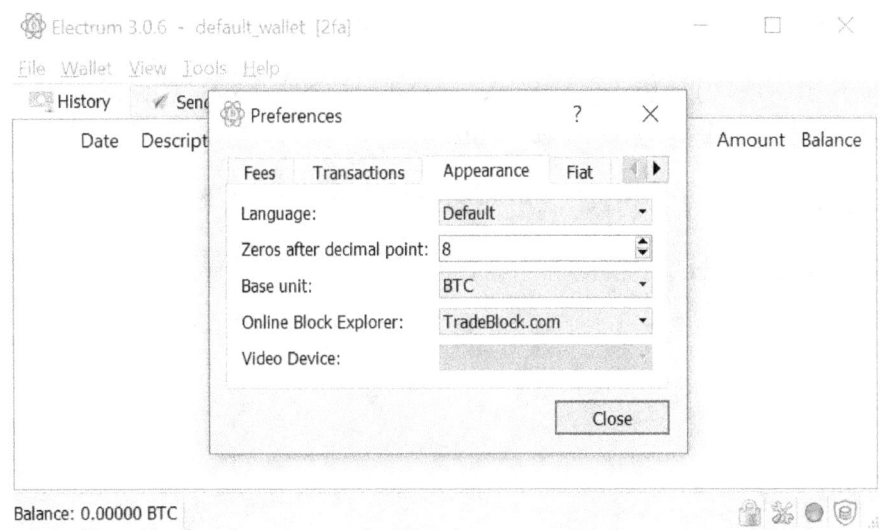

3. You can also select a fiat currency to know the market value of the bitcoin tokens. To enable this feature, go to the Fiat tab inside Preference. Then, pick your fiat currency preference and the source of the market value; for instance, Kraken or BitPay. If you are familiar with one of the source, you may pick that one – there will not be much difference in the prices updated live.

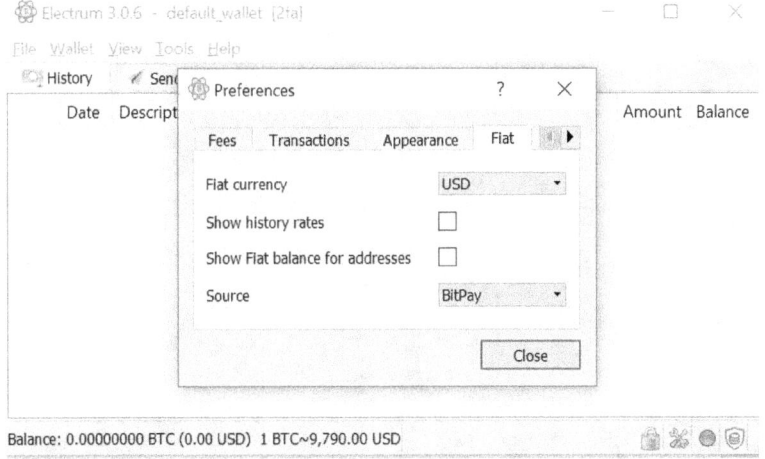

Now you are all set!

If you liked this information, you could tip to this BTC wallet I used to create the step-by-step tutorial:

3JoJ3GSzAJ2PMNUihx87G2cdHqtrURRXVk

It is safe to share BTC addresses.

How to sign up on Coinbase – exchange service for BTC, BCH, ETH, and LTC

Coinbase is one of the major exchanges in the USA with presence worldwide. Currently, Coinbase operates in Asia, Australia, Europe, and North America. You can check the currently available operations on this website. In this exchange, you can have wallets that support four of the top cryptocurrencies in the market, namely Bitcoin, Ethereum, Bitcoin Cash, and Litecoin.

Signing up on Coinbase is very simple. You will not need technical knowledge or experience of any kind. Furthermore, it takes no more than a few minutes to complete the registration. We will review the main steps to start buying and selling cryptocurrencies with this exchange.

1. First, go to the Coinbase website and click on the Sign-Up button at the right top corner of the web.

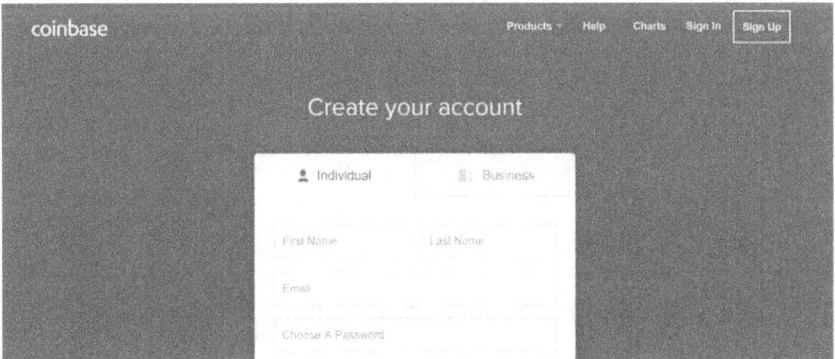

2. **Next, review the terms and user conditions that apply to this service.** It is essential to know the risks of using such exchange service provider. Although you will easily be able to change cryptocurrency tokens for fiat (once the verification of your identity is complete), you should understand that the reliability of the service conditions is NOT assured, e.g. delays

may occur due to technical or other reasons. Plus, if you do not protect the access to your account correctly, you risk losing your precious tokens. You should always keep in mind that saving a significant stake of tokens in this kind of accounts is not the best option.

> ☞ **How can you secure your tokens, then?** You can change fiat for cryptocurrency in an exchange, but you SHOULD store most of your token in desktop – or preferably hardware – the wallet. Having your tokens in an offline device which only connect to the internet to make a transaction is the best way to avoid security issues.

Better safe than sorry, right?

3. Once you have reviewed the User Agreement and the Privacy Policy, mark the tick box below the sign-up form.

☐ I certify that I am 18 years of age or older, and I agree to the User Agreement and Privacy Policy.

4. Complete your personal information and double check before clicking on the Create Account button. You will be required your First Name, Last Name, Email, and Password. You can make use of the Password Generator website to create a stable string as a password.

5. Have you checked your personal data? In that case, click on this button to proceed.

CREATE ACCOUNT

6. You will receive a verification mail where you will find a Verify Email Address link. Click on that button or follow the instructions in that email to complete this last step of the sign-

up process.

7. Next, you will need to complete the following steps to have an active account on Coinbase:

   i) Select the account type: individual or business.
   ii) Provide a telephone number (it is essential to have an accessible phone number for the security verification processes that may be necessary). The phone number allows you to carry out:
   a. Logins with two-step verification.
   b. Secure transactions.
   iii) Select a payment method to purchase cryptocurrency or to withdraw funds. This step requires verification and may take a few days to complete. Depending on the country you are based, you will see one or both usual options: a bank account and debit/credit card.
   iv) **ID verification.** Before you are fully able to make use of your Coinbase account, an identity verification process is required. You will be asked to provide one of the following documents: passport, driver's license or photo ID.
   This step can be completed by a webcam or a mobile camera. You can also attach scans of the documents in a compatible format, such as JPG or PDF.
   - **Mobile camera.** If you pick this option, you will receive a message with a link to upload the photo to your mobile. When you open this link, you will be directed to a page like this one:

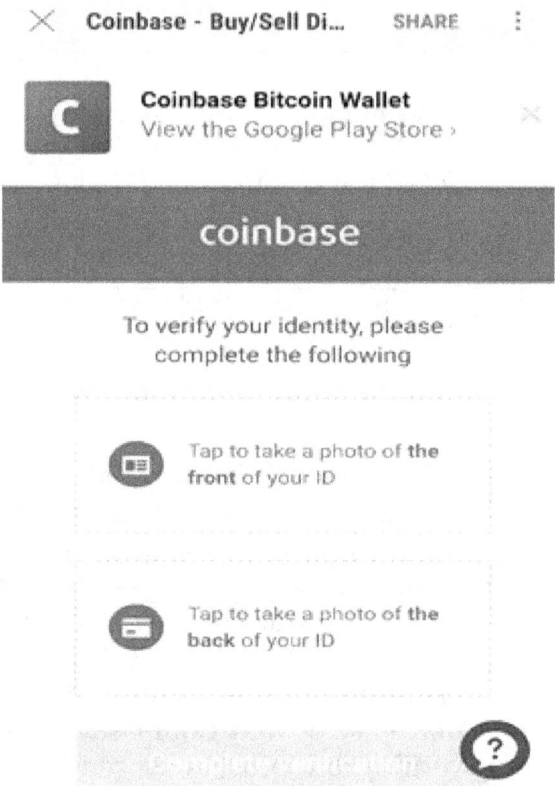

There, you can take pictures of your ID document and attach them instantly. When this step is complete, you will arrive at this page.

Cryptocurrency Masterclass 2018

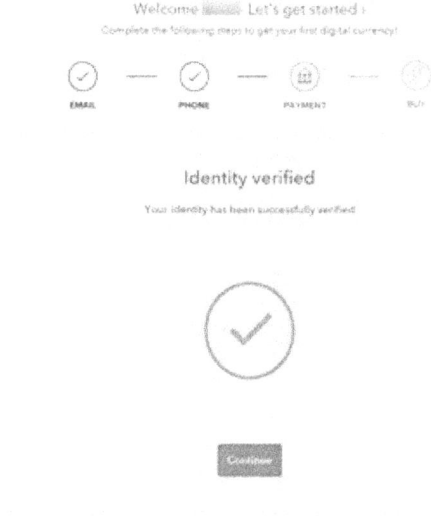

- **Webcam.** If you pick this option, you will receive instructions to scan your documents with the webcam of your computer. This option is as simple as the mobile camera ID process. In the end, you will be directed to the same verification page.

v) **Payment method.** Now, you will enter your payment information.

You will have to provide the following information to proceed:

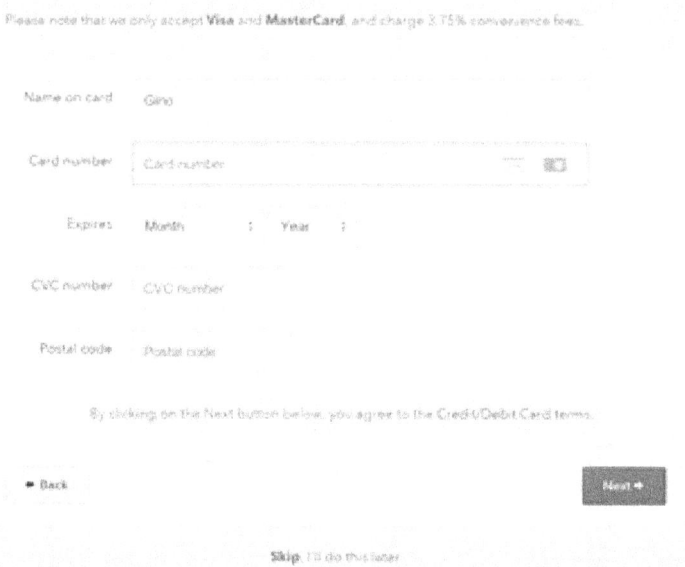

Also, you may skip this step to complete it later. If you picked a debit/credit card as the payment method, you would just need to complete the above form to proceed. The card will be validated within seconds.

To confirm a bank account, you will need to check your transactions historical, which appear as "Pending". There, you will see two small charges – you should input the two last digits (cents) of these charges to validate your bank account on Coinbase.

And we are all set! Yes, you just completed the sign-up process in a blast. Isn't that great?

Now, lets us review the basics about how to send and receive any supported cryptocurrency tokens. Please, **keep in mind that each of the wallets is uniquely meant to be used with the corresponding cryptocurrency**, e.g. sending BTC tokens to a BCH wallet will suppose the permanent loss of those tokens.

Read carefully about how to proceed with the use of the wallets supported by Coinbase, and always make small trials to understand the complete process of the transactions. You should not be concerned about issues with the wallets in the general case provided that the interface is user-friendly and straightforward.

How to receive BTC, ETH, BCH or LTC tokens on your Coinbase wallet

Please, not that it is safe to share cryptocurrency wallets publicly or directly with the person who will send you tokens.

Web

1. Log in to your Coinbase account to get started.

2. Next, go to Accounts.

3. Click on **Receive** in the cryptocurrency bar at the left side of the page.

4. You will see a reminder of the correct use of the wallet, i.e. only receive BTC tokens in the corresponding wallet. Just, click on **Show Address** to proceed.

5. Now, you will see the QR code for the selected address, and you will be able to copy the string to the clipboard to easily share the address, too. A BTC wallet may look like this:

3PZzasUuc25iufkP7op7xt5tfYtDEZRvWC

The QR code can be shared with a screenshot or by sharing the screen with the sender (be careful with sharing personal info, though). You can also post the wallet address on a website or with an HTML link.

As usual, it is safe to share an address because it only serves to receive tokens on your side.

Please, keep in mind that an ETH wallet on Coinbase **cannot** be used to receive mining rewards.

iOS

1. First, tap the QR icon in the upper right.
2. Then, tap **'My address'** near the top of the screen.
3. Now, allow the sender to scan your QR code or click **'Copy Address'** and send your address to the other party.

Android

1. First, tap the QR icon in the upper right.
2. Tap **'My address'** near the top of the screen.
3. Last, allow the sender to scan your QR code or click **'Copy Address'** and send your address to the other party.

How to send BTC, ETH, BCH or LTC tokens to another wallet on Coinbase

In this section, we review the main steps that you need to complete whenever you send tokens from any compatible device (web browser, Android, and iOS).

Web

1. Go to your personal account on the browser.

2. Then, select the **Send** button for the digital currency wallet that you'd like to send from. You can pick BTC, ETH, BCH or LTC.

3. Next, select the **Wallet Address** if you're sending to a digital currency wallet external to Coinbase or **Email Address** if you're sending via email. Always, make sure that the address you are sending to corresponds to the cryptocurrency you have selected. Likewise, double-check the e-mail address if you pick that option.

4. Enter the amount of digital currency you'd like to send in the **Amount** field. You can choose the number of tokens or it's corresponding value in your fiat currency. **Note that the funds will always be sent as digital currency, not your local currency.**

5. Click **Continue** to proceed.

6. Last, you will need to confirm the details of the transaction – make sure all the data is correct before you confirm this step. **There is no way of reversing the transaction, so the last step is a must-read.**

iOS

1. Tap the menu icon near the top left of the screen to open the **Navbar**.

2. Next, **select the wallet** you want to send from, which is located on the Navbar.

3. Now, tap the paper airplane icon in the upper right hand of the screen.

4. **Enter the number of tokens** you want to send. (Simply, tap the up/down arrows to switch between cryptocurrencies.)

5. Press **SEND** to make the transaction.

6. **Input the email or wallet address** and any notes you would like to include with the transaction.

7. Last, review the details of your transaction before tapping **'Send'** in the upper right corner of the screen. Now, the transaction is done.

QR code

1. First, tap the **QR icon** in the upper right.

2. Take a picture of the QR code you have been provided. Gently, move the camera to focus the QR code and make sure there is enough light to detect this code correctly.

3. Next, enter the desired number of tokens you want to send, and press **'Continue'** to proceed.

4. Last, double-check the details of your transaction before you tap **'Send'** in the upper right corner of the screen. Now, the transaction is complete on your side.

Android

1. First, tap the menu icon near the top left of the screen to open the Navbar.

2. Then, select the wallet you wish to send from, which will appear in the Navbar.

3. Now, tap the '+' icon near the lower right hand of the screen.

4. Tap **'Send'** to proceed.

5. Now, enter the number of tokens you'd like to send. (Tap the up/down arrows to switch between cryptocurrency selection.)

6. Also, enter the email or wallet address and include any notes you want to include in the transaction.

7. Last, double-check the details of your transaction and tap the **"forward"** arrow in the upper right corner of the screen to send the tokens. Now, the transaction is complete on your end.

QR code

1. First, tap the QR icon in the upper right.

2. Then, take a picture of the QR code you have been provided.

3. Now, enter the number of tokens and press **'Continue'** to proceed.

4. Last, double-check the details of your transaction and tap the **'forward'** arrow in the upper right corner of the screen. Now, the transaction is done on your side.